FRENCH

Verbs &

Essentials
of Grammar

Second Edition

Simone Oudot

New York Chicago San Francisco Lisbon London Madrid Mexico City
Milan New Delhi San Juan Seoul Singapore Sydney Toronto

Copyright © 2008 by The McGraw-Hill Companies, Inc. All rights reserved. Printed in the
United States of America. Except as permitted under the United States Copyright Act of
1976, no part of this publication may be reproduced or distributed in any form or by any
means, or stored in a database or retrieval system, without the prior written permission of
the publisher.

1 2 3 4 5 6 7 8 9 10 11 12 13 14 15 16 17 18 19   CUS/CUS   0 9 8 7

ISBN 978-0-07-149804-3
MHID   0-07-149804-4

McGraw-Hill books are available at special quantity discounts to use as premiums and
sales promotions, or for use in corporate training programs. For more information, please
write to the Director of Special Sales, Professional Publishing, McGraw-Hill, Two Penn
Plaza, New York, NY 10121-2298. Or contact your local bookstore.

This book is printed on acid-free paper.

Preface

French Verbs and Essentials of Grammar is a practical handbook and guide to the principal grammatical concepts of the French language for learners at any level of proficiency. Concepts are presented in a logical order and concise manner so that students with no more than one semester of French can follow the explanations. More advanced students—even those who have gained considerable mastery—will find this an excellent quick reference, study and review guide, or grammatical brush-up aid. This book can be used as a basis for group work, individual study, or simply as a classroom or personal reference.

Part I focuses on the mastery of French verbs. The chapter on pronunciation at the beginning of the section gives a good introduction for beginners to the sounds of the language. In subsequent chapters, all tenses and conjugations of verbs are presented, with extensive, easy-to-use verb charts and clear explanations. Correct use of tense and mood as well as sequence of tenses are also covered in this section. In this way, learners master correct usage, as well as simply learn to conjugate verbs.

Part II presents concise explanations of other essential points of French grammar, including articles, pronouns, interrogatives and exclamations, prepositions, and much more. The examples chosen to illustrate each concept were selected for authenticity. They are phrases and sentences frequently used in contemporary, idiomatic French, providing clear illustrations of current usage.

For classwork or for personal reference, *French Verbs and Essentials of Grammar* is a versatile and easy-to-use guide to French grammar. It is a useful tool for learners seeking not only to learn verb tenses and grammar points but also to master correct usage. For learners at any level, *French Verbs and Essentials of Grammar* can help pave the way to mastery of the French language.

Contents

Part One:
French Verbs

1. Pronunciation

There are 37 sounds in French corresponding to 37 symbols of the International Phonetic Alphabet.

Vowels

[i]   il, vie, Sylvie
[a]   patte, carte
[ɑ]   pâte, basse
[ɛ]   tête, bête, laide, merci
[e]   blé, quai
[c]   sotte, robe

[o]   dôme, sot, beau, gauche
[u]   cou, roue
[y]   mur, vendu, eu
[ə]   le, fenêtre, je
[œ]   œuf, jeune, peur
[o]   feu, creux, œufs

Nasals

[ã]   an, Jean, lent
[ɛ̃]   pin, pain, plein

[ɔ̃]   bon, rond, ombre
[œ̃]   un, brun, lundi

Consonants

[p]   pas, prix, soupe
[t]   tôt, très, vite
[k]   cas, qui, kilo, sac
[f]   feu, photo, neuf
[s]   sel, dessous, sceau, nation, ceux
[ʃ]   chaud, chemin, tâche
[b]   bateau, beurre, rabais
[d]   dent, direction, aide
[g]   Gabriel, gâteau, bague

[v]   vin, rêve,
[z]   rose, désert, zéro
[ʒ]   neige, jaune
[l]   là, lune, sol
[r]   rat, rire, venir
[m]   mal, méchant, dame
[n]   nez, nid, sonner
[ɲ]   montagne, chataigne
[ŋ]   camping, parking

Semi-Consonants

[j]   yeux, soleil, pied
[w]   oui, moi, ouate

[ɥ]   huile, cuire

The Alphabet

a	[a]	h	[aʃ]	o	[o]	v	[ve]
b	[be]	i	[i]	p	[pe]	w	[dublə-ve]
c	[se]	j	[ʒi]	q	[ky]	x	[iks]
d	[de]	k	[ka]	r	[er]	y	[i-grɛk]
e	[ə]	l	[el]	s	[ɛs]	z	[zed]
f	[ɛf]	m	[em]	t	[te]		
g	[ge]	n	[en]	u	[y]		

Accents

′	l'accent aigu	é gives the sound	[e]
`	l'accent grave	è gives the sound	[e]
^	l'accent circonflexe	ê gives the sound	[e]
••	le tréma Noël	[noel]	

1. *Le tréma* means that the preceding vowel must be pronounced separately.

2. The *accent grave* over *a* and *u* does not affect the sound of the vowels: *à* [a]; *où* [u].

3. The *accent circonflexe* over *a* affects the sound of this vowel slightly, sometimes not, depending on the speaker's dialect.

château = [ʃato]   or [ʃɑto]

Rhythm and Intonation

1. In French, syllables are not stressed as they are in English. Instead, there tends to be a slight stress on the last syllable of a sentence or phrase. As a result, each syllable has equal length, except the last one, but the pause is very slight.

Nous allons déjeuner.
Nous allons déjeuner chez Suzanne.
Après les courses, nous allons déjeuner chez Suzanne.
Après les courses, mon mari et moi, nous allons déjeuner chez Suzanne.

2. In general, the intonation in French is dictated by the speaker's feelings. However, a general rule is that there is a falling intonation at the end of an affirmative or a negative sentence. In interrogative sentences, there is falling intonation at the end of a question asking for information and rising intonation at the end of a yes/no question.

Où vas-tu?

Veux-tu du lait?

Qu'est-ce que tu fais?

Irez-vous dans les Alpes cette année?

Comment va votre mère?

Est-ce que tu as réussi à ton examen?

Punctuation Marks

,	la virgule	!	le point d'exclamation
.	le point	( )	la parenthèse
:	les deux points	≪ ≫	les guillemets
;	le point virgule	'	l'apostrophe
. . .	les points de suspension	-	le trait d'union
?	le point d'interrogation	—	le tiret

Punctuation in French is much the same as in English, with some differences.

1. *Les guillemets* ≪   ≫ replace English quotation marks.

Comme La Fontaine l'a dit:≪Rien ne sert de courir, il faut partir à point≫.	As La Fontaine said: "It's no use to run, if you did not start on time."

2. A dash (*tiret*) is used to set off the words spoken by different speakers in a dialogue.

— Il fait beau, dit Paul. On sort?	"The weather is good," said Paul. "Shall we go out?"

2. Regular Verbs — The Simple Tense Forms

The Infinitive

Regular French verbs are classed according to the endings of the infinitive: the first conjugation (verbs whose infinitives end in -er); the second conjugation (-ir verbs); and the third conjugation (-re verbs). -Er verbs constitute a majority of French verbs.

parler to speak   **finir** to finish   **vendre** to sell

When the ending of the infinitive is dropped, what is left is called the stem. The sets of endings that are added to the stem or to the infinitive to denote person, number, tense, and mood are called conjugations.

Simple Tenses of the Indicative Mood

1. Present   **Le présent**
2. Imperfect   **L'imparfait**
3. Simple Past   **Le passé simple**
4. Future   **Le futur**

Conditional Mood

5. Present Conditional   **Le présent du conditionnel**

Imperative Mood

6. Imperative   **Le présent de l'impératif**

Subject Pronouns

For a detailed discussion of subject pronouns, see Chapter 20. Remember that the subject of the verb is of first, second, or third person, singular or plural.

	Singular		Plural	
1st person	**je (j')**	I	**nous**	we
2nd person	**tu**	you	**vous** (formal singular)	you
			vous (plural)	you
3rd person	**il**	he	**ils** *(m.)*	they
	elle	she	**elles** *(f.)*	they
	on	one, we, they, people		

The Present

First Conjugation, -*er* Verbs

The present tense expresses an action or a state that is taking place at the moment of speech. There is a difference in the notion of time between English and French. While French expresses time at the precise moment the action is taking place, English most often acknowledges the duration of the action. *Je parle français* is the equivalent of both "I am speaking French" and "I speak French." English also uses an emphatic expression, *I do speak,* which does not exist in French.

The present tense in French is formed by adding the appropriate endings to the stem of the infinitive.

parler, to speak

je parl*e*	I speak, am speaking	**nous parl***ons*	we speak, are speaking
tu parl*es*	you speak, are speaking	**vous parl***ez*	you speak, are speaking
il parl*e*	he speaks, is speaking	**ils parl***ent*	they speak, are speaking
elle parl*e*	she speaks, is speaking	**elles parl***ent*	they speak, are speaking
on parl*e*	we, they, people speak, are speaking; one speaks		

A noun, pronoun, or a combination of a noun and a pronoun may be used as the subject of the verb form.

Je parle **français.**	I speak French. I do speak French.
Anne et moi, nous parlons **anglais.**	Anne and I speak English.
Elles parlent **à Paul.**	They are speaking to Paul.
Les enfants parlent **mal.**	The children speak badly.
On parle **des vacances.**	We are talking about vacation.

Negative Form

To form the negative, place *ne* (*n'*) before the verb and *pas* after the verb. (See Chapter 24.)

Je *ne* **parle** *pas* **espagnol.**	I don't speak Spanish.
Tu *ne* **parles** *pas* **bien.**	You are not speaking well.
On *ne* **parle** *pas* **de toi.**	We are not talking about you.

Sample Verbs of the First Conjugation

aider to help	**monter** to go up, to climb
aimer to love, to like	**montrer** to show
apporter to bring	**oublier** to forget
arriver to arrive	**parler** to speak, to talk
chanter to sing	**passer** to pass
commencer to begin, to start	**penser** to think
demander to ask	**porter** to carry, to wear
donner to give	**préparer** to prepare
entrer to enter, to go in	**raconter** to tell
étudier to study	**regarder** to look at
fermer to close	**rester** to stay
habiter to live	**tourner** to turn
inviter to invite	**travailler** to work
jouer to play	**trouver** to find

Second Conjugation, -*ir* Verbs

finir, to finish
I finish, am finishing, etc.

Singular		Plural	
je fin*is*		**nous fin***issons*	
tu fin*is*		**vous fin***issez*	
il		**ils**	
elle	**fin***it*	**elles**	**fin***issent*
on			

Je *finis* **mes devoirs.**	I am finishing my homework.
Jean *finit* **son repas.**	Jean is finishing his meal.
Où *finissez*-**vous vos vacances?**	Where are you ending your vacation?
Nous *finissons* **nos achats.**	We are finishing our shopping.
Elles *finissent* **leur voyage à Rome.**	They are finishing their trip in Rome.

Sample Verbs of the Second Conjugation

atterrir to land	**languir** to languish
brunir to brown, to tan	**maigrir** to grow thin
démolir to demolish, to pull down	**obéir** to obey
élargir to widen	**pourrir** to rot
finir to finish	**raccourcir** to shorten
fleurir to bloom	**ralentir** to slow down
gémir to groan, to moan	**réfléchir** to think over
grandir to grow tall	**remplir** to fill, to fill out
grossir to grow bigger	**réunir** to gather
guérir to recover	**réussir** to succeed
investir to invest	**rôtir** to roast

Third Conjugation, -*re* Verbs

vendre, to sell
I sell, am selling, etc.

Singular	Plural
je vend*s*	**nous vend***ons*
tu vend*s*	**vous vend***ez*
il (elle, on) vend	**ils (elles) vend***ent*

Je *vends* **ma maison.**	I am selling my house.
Vendez-**vous du beurre?**	Do you sell butter?
Nous *vendons* **aussi des œufs.**	We also sell eggs.
Elles *vendent* **des écharpes.**	They sell scarves.
Ils ne *vendent* **rien.**	They sell nothing.

Sample Verbs of the Third Conjugation

attendre	to wait for	**pondre**	to lay (eggs)
défendre	to defend, to forbid	**répandre**	to spread, to spill
descendre	to go down	**répondre**	to answer
entendre	to hear	**rendre**	to give back
épandre	to spread	**tendre**	to stretch
fondre	to melt	**tondre**	to shear, to mow (grass)
mordre	to bite	**vendre**	to sell
pendre	to hang		

Sample Present Tense Sentences

Je *travaille* **dans un bureau.**	I work in an office.
Alice *vend* **sa voiture.**	Alice is selling her car.
Nous ne *regardons* **pas la télévision.**	We are not watching television.
Comment *trouvez*-**vous Jacques?**	How do you like Jacques?
Ils *montent* **au premier.**	They are going up to the second floor.
Les Dupont n'*habitent* **pas à Nice.**	The Duponts do not live in Nice.
Josette *obéit* **à ses parents.**	Josette obeys her parents.
Vous *jouez* **au bridge?**	Do you play bridge?
Tu *portes* **une jolie robe.**	You are wearing a pretty dress.
Elles nous *invitent* **à rester.**	They invite us to stay.

The Imperfect

There are two simple past tenses in French, the imperfect (*imparfait*) and the simple past (*passé simple*). Their uses vary.

The imperfect is the tense of description. It describes an action or a state that took place in the past, without defining its duration or its time of completion.

Il *habitait* **Londres pendant la guerre.**	He lived in London during the war.

But when one indicates the duration, another past tense must be used (*passé composé* or *passé simple*).

Il *a habité* (*il habita*) **Londres pendant dix ans.**	He lived in London for ten years.

The imperfect is also used to express a habitual action or an action that occurred repeatedly in the past.

Elle *tondait* **la pelouse tous les jours.**	She mowed the lawn every day.

The imperfect is used to describe physical or mental states that existed in the past.

Il *avait* **mal à la tête et ne se** *souvenait* **de rien.**	He had a headache and remembered nothing.

The imperfect tense is formed by adding the appropriate endings to the first person plural of the indicative tense (minus the -*ons*).

parler (*parlons*)
I was speaking, used to speak, etc.

je parlais	**nous parl**ions
tu parlais	**vous parl**iez
il (elle, on) parlait	**ils (elles) parl**aient

finir (*finissons*)
I was finishing, used to finish, etc.

je finissais	**nous finiss**ions
tu finissais	**vous finiss**iez
il (elle, on) finissait	**ils (elles) finiss**aient

vendre (*vendons*)
I was selling, used to sell, etc.

je vendais	**nous vend**ions
tu vendais	**vous vend**iez
il (elle, on) vendait	**ils (elles) vend**aient

Je *demandais* **son adresse.**	I was asking his address.
Il *travaillait* **dur.**	He was working hard.
Nous *parlions* **de vous.**	We were talking about you.
Alice et Jacqueline *obéissaient* **toujours.**	Alice and Jacqueline obeyed always.
Vous *défendiez* **les pauvres.**	You used to defend poor people.
C'est le bruit que nous *entendions*.	That's the noise we used to hear.

See Chapter 10, Sequence of Tenses (page 47), for an explanation of the uses of the *imparfait* versus the *passé composé*.

The Passé Simple

The *passé simple* (simple past tense) expresses an action or a state that occurred at a specific time in the past. It is used only in writing and is usually found in literature. Its equivalent in conversation is the *passé composé*, a perfect tense. (See Chapter 3.)

The simple past tense is formed by adding the appropriate endings to the stem of the infinitive.

parler		**finir**	
I spoke, did speak, etc.		I finished, did finish, etc.	
je parl*ai*	nous parl*âmes*	je fin*is*	nous fin*îmes*
tu parl*as*	vous parl*âtes*	tu fin*is*	vous fin*îtes*
il (elle, on) parl*a*	ils (elles) parl*èrent*	il (elle, on) fin*it*	ils (elles) fin*irent*

vendre	
I sold, did sell, etc.	
je vend*is*	nous vend*îmes*
tu vend*is*	vous vend*îtes*
il (elle, on) vend*it*	ils (elles) vend*irent*

Je me *préparai* à partir.	I prepared myself to leave.
Il *entra* sans frapper.	He came in without knocking.
Nous *perdîmes* notre chemin.	We lost our way.
Les lilas *fleurirent* tôt.	The lilacs bloomed early.
Les voitures *passèrent* à toute vitesse.	The cars passed by at high speed.

The Future

The future tense is formed by adding the future endings to the infinitive of *-er* and *-ir* verbs. For *-re* verbs, the *e* is dropped before adding the endings.

parler		**finir**	
I will speak, etc.		I will finish, etc.	
je parler*ai*	nous parler*ons*	je finir*ai*	nous finir*ons*
tu parler*as*	vous parler*ez*	tu finir*as*	vous finir*ez*
il (elle, on) parler*a*	ils (elles) parler*ont*	il (elle, on) finir*a*	ils (elles) finir*ont*

vendre	
I will sell, etc.	
je vendr*ai*	nous vendr*ons*
tu vendr*as*	vous vendr*ez*
il (elle, on) vendr*a*	ils (elles) vendr*ont*

J'*apporterai* les sandwichs.	I'll bring the sandwiches.
Tu *étudieras* tout l'été.	You'll study all summer.
Les fruits *pourriront*.	The fruits will rot.
Nous *réfléchirons* à votre proposition.	We'll think about your proposal.
Vous *défendrez* votre pays.	You'll defend your country.

The Conditional Mood

The endings of the present conditional are, like those of the future tense, added to the whole infinitive.

parler
I would speak, etc.

je parler*ais*	nous parler*ions*
tu parler*ais*	vous parler*iez*
il (elle, on) parler*ait*	ils (elles) parler*aient*

finir
I would finish, etc.

je finir*ais*	nous finir*ions*
tu finir*ais*	vous finir*iez*
il (elle, on) finir*ait*	ils (elles) finir*aient*

vendre
I would sell, etc.

je vendr*ais*	nous vendr*ions*
tu vendr*ais*	vous vendr*iez*
il (elle, on) vendr*ait*	ils (elles) vendr*aient*

1. The conditional usually expresses an eventuality. The cause or condition for this eventuality can be implicit or explicit.

The eventuality can be contained in a *si*-clause, in which case it is explicit.

Si tu parlais plus fort, on t'entendrait.	If you spoke louder, we would hear you.
Je grossirais si je mangeais plus.	I would put on weight if I ate more.
Si vous m'invitiez, je resterais.	If you invited me, I would stay.

When the eventuality is implied in the conditional clause, the cause and condition are implicit.

Aimeriez-vous être balayeur de rues?	Would you like to be a street sweeper?
Auriez-vous l'audace de m'accuser de voler?	Would you be so audacious as to accuse me of stealing?

2. The conditional is also used to make a request or a refusal more polite.

J'aimerais te parler.	I would like to speak to you.
Je ne voudrais pas la voir.	I would not want to see her.

3. The conditional also expresses probability or conjecture.

Il vendrait sa maison.	He is probably selling his house.
Est-ce qu'elle l'achèterait?	Would she buy it?

The Imperative Mood

The imperative takes its forms from the second person singular of the indicative present (verbs in -*er* drop the -s) and from the first and second person plural of the indicative present. The imperative is a mood of action. It is used to command or persuade, with the intent of prompting a result.

parler	finir	vendre
parle	finis	vends
parlons	finissons	vendons
parlez	finissez	vendez

Parle à ton voisin!	Speak to your neighbor!
Finissons notre travail!	Let's finish our work!
Vendez votre voiture à Charles!	Sell your car to Charles!

Endings of Simple Tenses

Indicative Mood

	-er		-ir		-re	
Present	*stem* e	___ ons	___ is	___ issons	___ s	___ ons
	___ es	___ ez	___ is	___ issez	___ s	___ ez
	___ e	___ ent	___ it	___ issent	___	___ ent
Imperfect	___ ais	___ ions	___ ais	___ ions	___ ais	___ ions
	___ ais	___ iez	___ ais	___ iez	___ ais	___ iez
	___ ait	___ aient	___ ait	___ aient	___ ait	___ aient
Passé Simple	___ ai	___ âmes	___ is	___ îmes	___ is	___ îmes
	___ as	___ âtes	___ is	___ îtes	___ is	___ îtes
	___ a	___ èrent	___ it	___ irent	___ it	___ irent

Future	*infinitive* ai	___ ons
	___ as	___ ez
	___ a	___ ont

Conditional Mood

Present	*infinitive* ais	___ ions
	___ ais	___ iez
	___ ait	___ aient

Imperative Mood

Present	___ e	___ is	___ s
	___ ons	___ issons	___ ons
	___ ez	___ issez	___ ez

Verb Synopsis

In a synopsis any one form of the verb is given in all the tenses.

parler - je

Indicative	Simple Tenses	Translation
Present	**je parle**	I speak, I am speaking
Imperfect	**je parlais**	I used to speak, was speaking
Passé Simple	**je parlai**	I spoke
Future	**je parlerai**	I will speak
Conditional Present	**je parlerais**	I would speak
Imperative (*tu* form)	**parle!**	speak!

3. Regular Verbs — Auxiliary Verbs and the Perfect Tenses

The perfect (compound) tenses are formed with a simple tense form of one of the auxiliary verbs (*avoir* or *être*) and a past participle.

The perfect tenses are:

1. Present Perfect   Le passé composé
2. Pluperfect   Le plus-que-parfait
3. Preterite Perfect   Le passé antérieur
4. Future Perfect   Le futur antérieur
5. Past Conditional   Le conditionnel passé

Simple Tenses of *Avoir* and *Être*

avoir	Present	Imperfect	Passé Simple
to have	j'ai	j'avais	j'eus
	tu as	tu avais	tu eus
	il (elle, on) a	il (elle, on) avait	il (elle, on) eut
	nous avons	nous avions	nous eûmes
	vous avez	vous aviez	vous eûtes
	ils (elles) ont	ils (elles) avaient	ils (elles) eurent

	Future	Conditional
	j'aurai	j'aurais
	tu auras	tu aurais
	il (elle, on) aura	il (elle, on) aurait
	nous aurons	nous aurions
	vous aurez	vous auriez
	ils (elles) auront	ils (elles) auraient

être	Present	Imperfect	Passé Simple
to be	je suis	j'étais	je fus
	tu es	tu étais	tu fus
	il (elle, on) est	il (elle, on) était	il (elle, on) fut
	nous sommes	nous étions	nous fûmes
	vous êtes	vous étiez	vous fûtes
	ils (elles) sont	ils (elles) étaient	ils (elles) furent

	Future	Conditional
	je serai	je serais
	tu seras	tu serais
	il (elle, on) sera	il (elle, on) serait
	nous serons	nous serions
	vous serez	vous seriez
	ils (elles) seront	ils (elles) seraient

The auxiliary verb *avoir* is used with the majority of verbs.

J'*ai* mangé une pomme.   I ate an apple.
Nous *avons* maigri cette année.   We lost weight this year.

However, the following verbs take the auxiliary *être*. Nearly all these verbs describe motion.

Infinitive	Past participle
aller to go	allé
arriver to arrive, to happen	arrivé
descendre to go down, to come down	descendu
devenir to become	devenu
entrer to enter, to go in	entré
monter to climb, to go up	monté
mourir to die	mort
naître to be born	né
partir to leave	parti
rentrer to go back, to go home	rentré
rester to stay, to remain	resté
retourner to return	retourné
revenir to come back	revenu
sortir to go out	sorti
tomber to fall	tombé
venir to come	venu

Elle *est* tombée dans l'escalier.   She fell in the stairs.
Il *est né* le premier décembre.   He was born on December 1st.

The verbs *descendre, monter, rentrer,* and *sortir,* when used as transitive verbs (which take a direct object), are conjugated with *avoir.*

Nous *avons descendu* les valises.   We took the suitcases downstairs.

The Past Participle

A past participle is formed by adding -*é* to the stem of an -*er* verb, -*i* to the stem of an -*ir* verb, and -*u* to the stem of an -*re* verb.

parl*er*	**parl*é***	spoken, talked
fin*ir*	**fin*i***	finished
vend*re*	**vend*u***	sold

NOTE: See Chapter 8, Irregular Verbs, for irregular past participles.

The Passé Composé

The *passé composé* is formed with the present tense of *avoir* or *être* and a past participle. It is used to describe an action or a state that happened in the past at a precise moment. See Chapter 10, Sequence of Tenses, for an explanation of the *imparfait* versus the *passé composé.*

parler I spoke, I talked, etc.

j'ai parlé	**nous avons parlé**
tu as parlé	**vous avez parlé**
il (elle, on) a parlé	**ils (elles) ont parlé**

sortir I went out, etc.

je suis sorti(e)	**nous sommes sorti(e)s**
tu es sorti(e)	**vous êtes sorti(e)(s)**
il (elle, on) est sorti(e)	**ils (elles) sont sorti(e)s**

Il m'a donné un cadeau.	He gave me a present.
Vous êtes allés en Italie.	You went to Italy.

NOTE: In compound tenses, the negative is placed on either side of the auxiliary verb.

Nous *n'***avons** *pas* **vendu la voiture.**   We did not sell the car.

Agreement with the Past Participle

Verbs Using *Avoir* as the Auxiliary

If a verb is conjugated with *avoir,* the past participle agrees with the direct object, *if* the direct object precedes the verb. The direct object can be a personal pronoun, the relative pronoun *que* at the beginning of a relative clause, or the interrogative or exclamative pronouns *quel* or *lequel.*

Où sont mes lunettes? Tu *les* **as** **pos***ées* **sur la table.**	Where are my glasses? You put them on the table.
Thérèse? Oui, c'est *elle* **que j'ai** **invit***ée.*	Thérèse? Yes, it is she that I invited.
Quels *fruits* **as-tu mang***és***?**	What fruits did you eat?

Verbs Using *Être* as the Auxiliary

If the verb is conjugated with *être,* the past participle agrees with the subject of the verb.

Elle **est parti***e* **à cinq heures.**	She left at five.
Nous **étions arriv***és* **à l'heure.**	We had gotten there on time.
Marc **sera allé chez moi.**	Marc will have gone to my home.

The Pluperfect

The *plus-que-parfait* is formed with the imperfect of *avoir* or *être* and a past participle.

parler I had spoken, etc.

j'avais parlé	nous avions parlé
tu avais parlé	vous aviez parlé
il (elle, on) avait parlé	ils (elles) avaient parlé

venir I had come, etc.

j'étais venu(e)	nous étions venu(e)s
tu étais venu(e)	vous étiez venu(e)(s)
il (elle) était venu(e)	ils (elles) étaient venu(e)s

Jean a dit qu'il t'avait donné son livre.	Jean said that he had given you his book.
Les Martin avaient déjà dîné.	The Martins had already eaten.
Elle était entrée sans frapper.	She had gone in without knocking.

The Preterite Perfect

This tense is formed with the *passé simple* of *être* or *avoir* and a past participle. Like the *passé simple*, this tense is used only in literary works.

finir I finished, etc.

j'eus fini	nous eûmes fini
tu eus fini	vous eûtes fini
il (elle, on) eut fini	ils (elles) eurent fini

aller I went, etc.

je fus allé(e)	nous fûmes allé(e)s
tu fus allé(e)	vous fûtes allé(e)(s)
il (elle, on) fut allé(e)	ils (elles) furent allé(e)s

Quand j'eus fini de parler, ils entrèrent.	When I had stopped speaking, they came in.
Nous fûmes arrivés avant tous les autres.	We arrived before everybody else.

The Future Perfect

The future perfect is formed with the future of *être* or *avoir* and a past participle.

vendre I will have sold, etc.

j'aurai vendu	nous aurons vendu
tu auras vendu	vous aurez vendu
il (elle, on) aura vendu	ils (elles) auront vendu

arriver I will have arrived, etc.

je serai arrivé(e)	nous serons arrivé(e)s
tu seras arrivé(e)	vous serez arrivé(e)(s)
il (elle, on) sera arrivé(e)	ils (elles) seront arrivé(e)s

J'aurai fini mes valises à huit heures.	I will have finished my suitcases at eight o'clock.
Nous serons partis avant minuit.	We will be gone before midnight.

NOTE: The future perfect is also used to express probability or conjecture, referring to the past.

Il aura sans doute appelé.	He has probably called.
Elles seront sorties sans leurs chapeaux.	They probably went out without their hats.

The Past Conditional

The past conditional is formed with the conditional of *avoir* or *être* and a past participle.

ralentir I would have slowed down, etc.

j'aurais ralenti	nous aurions ralenti
tu aurais ralenti	vous auriez ralenti
il (elle, on) aurait ralenti	ils (elles) auraient ralenti

devenir I would have become, etc.

je serais devenu(e)	nous serions devenu(e)s
tu serais devenu(e)	vous seriez devenu(e)(s)
il (elle, on) serait devenu(e)	ils (elles) seraient devenu(e)s

J'aurais ralenti si j'avais vu l'agent de police.	I would have slowed down if I had seen the policeman.
Il serait mort d'asphyxie.	He would have died of asphyxiation.

NOTE: The conditional perfect is also used to express probability or conjecture, referring to the past.

Il aurait sans doute appelé.	He would probably have called.
Il serait peut-être arrivé à le faire.	He would perhaps have succeeded in doing it.

Perfect Tenses

Avoir Plus Past Participle

Passé Composé	ai + *past participle*	avons _____
	as _____	avez _____
	a _____	ont _____
Plus-que-parfait	avais _____	avions _____
	avais _____	aviez _____
	avait _____	avaient _____

Preterite Perfect	eus _____	eûmes _____
	eus _____	eûtes _____
	eut _____	eurent _____
Future Perfect	aurai _____	aurons _____
	auras _____	aurez _____
	aura _____	auront _____
Past Conditional	aurais _____	aurions _____
	aurais _____	auriez _____
	aurait _____	auraient _____

Être Plus Past Participle

Passé Composé	suis *past participle*	sommes _____
	es _____	êtes _____
	est _____	sont _____
Plus-que-parfait	étais _____	étions _____
	étais _____	étiez _____
	était _____	étaient _____
Preterite Perfect	fus _____	fûmes _____
	fus _____	fûtes _____
	fut _____	furent _____
Future Perfect	serai _____	serons _____
	seras _____	serez _____
	sera _____	seront _____
Past Conditional	serais _____	serions _____
	serais _____	seriez _____
	serait _____	seraient _____

Synopsis of the Perfect Tenses

parler - je

Passé Composé	j'ai parlé	I have spoken, I spoke
Pluperfect	j'avais parlé	I had spoken
Preterite Perfect	j'eus parlé	I had spoken
Future Perfect	j'aurai parlé	I will have spoken
Past Conditional	j'aurais parlé	I would have spoken

aller - je

Passé Composé	je suis allé(e)	I have gone, I went
Pluperfect	j'étais allé(e)	I had gone
Preterite Perfect	je fus allé(e)	I had gone
Future Perfect	je serai allé(e)	I will have gone
Past Conditional	je serais allé(e)	I would have gone

4. Pronominal Verbs

A pronominal verb is composed of a reflexive pronoun and a verb. Pronominal verbs are used frequently in French. The reflexive pronouns are *me, te, se, nous, vous, se.* The reflexive pronoun in the infinitive is *se.*

Reflexive Verbs

A reflexive verb is one in which the subject and the object of the verb represent the same person. That is, the subject acts upon itself.

s'habiller to get dressed

Present
I get dressed (dress myself), etc.

je m'habille	**nous nous habillons**
tu t'habilles	**vous vous habillez**
il (elle, on) s'habille	**ils (elles) s'habillent**

Je me lève à sept heures.	I get up at seven o'clock.
Nous nous préparons à sortir.	We are getting ready to go out.
Les garçons **se promènent** sur la plage.	The boys are walking on the beach.

NOTE: The negative *ne* always comes before the reflexive pronoun and *pas* after the verb.

Vous *ne* **vous arrêtez** *pas* à Lyon?	Aren't you stopping in Lyon?

With inversion, the reflexive pronoun precedes the verb.

Vous **reposez-vous?**	Are you resting?

Compound Tenses

All reflexive verbs take *être* as the auxiliary in compound tenses. The reflexive pronoun immediately precedes *être,* and the past participle agrees in number and gender with the subject.

Suzanne, à quelle heure t'es-tu lev*ée* ce matin?	Suzanne, at what time did you get up this morning?
Nos parents s'étaient dépêchés.	Our parents hurried up.
Mes cousines se seraient bien amus*ées*.	My cousins would have enjoyed themselves.

NOTE: The negative *ne* always comes before the reflexive pronoun and *pas* after the auxiliary verb.

Ils *ne* se seront *pas* rencontrés avant midi.	They will not have met before noon.

Reciprocal Verbs

A reciprocal verb is used when the action passes from one person or thing to another, or from one group to another. It is only used in the first and third persons plural.

Nous nous sommes battus.	We fought each other.
Elles se sont entendues.	They got along together.

Some Verbs that Change Meaning When Used Pronominally

agir to act, to behave		**s'agir de** to be about	
aller to go		**s'en aller** to go away	
amuser to amuse (someone else)		**s'amuser** to enjoy oneself, to have a good time	
appeler to call		**s'appeler** to be called, to be named	
asseoir to seat		**s'asseoir** to sit down	
battre to beat		**se battre** to fight	
demander to ask		**se demander** to wonder	
endormir to put to sleep		**s'endormir** to fall asleep	
ennuyer to annoy		**s'ennuyer** to get bored	
lever to raise, to lift		**se lever** to get up	
passer to pass, to spend (time)		**se passer** to happen	
		se passer de to do without	
rappeler to call back		**se rappeler** to recall, to remember	
retourner to return, to go back		**se retourner** to turn around	
vanter to praise		**se vanter** to boast	

NOTE: When a reflexive verb is used with a part of the body, there is no agreement of the past participle.

Il s'est lavé les dents.	He brushed his teeth.
Elle s'est cassé le cou.	She broke her neck.

5. Formation of Subjunctive Tenses

The subjunctive is the mood of uncertainty and emotion, and usually is used to reflect the speaker's attitude. The subjunctive occurs most frequently in dependent clauses introduced by *que*. (The varied uses of the subjunctive will be explained in Chapter 6.) There are four tenses of the subjunctive. The first two tenses are commonly used in everyday speech; the second two are used only in writing.

NOTE: The subjunctive forms of irregular verbs are included in Chapter 8.

Subjunctive Tenses

Present	Le présent
Past	Le passé
Imperfect	L'imparfait
Pluperfect	Le plus-que-parfait

Present Subjunctive

The regular present subjunctive is formed by adding the endings *-e, -es, -e, -ions, -iez, ent* to the *ils* (third person plural) form of the present indicative (drop the *-ent*).

parler

que je parl*e*	que nous parl*ions*
que tu parl*es*	que vous parl*iez*
qu'il (elle, on) parl*e*	qu'ils (elles) parl*ent*

finir

que je finiss*e*	que nous finiss*ions*
que tu finiss*es*	que vous finiss*iez*
qu'il (elle, on) finiss*e*	qu'ils (elles) finiss*ent*

vendre

que je vend*e*	que nous vend*ions*
que tu vend*es*	que vous vend*iez*
qu'il (elle, on) vend*e*	qu'ils (elles) vend*ent*

Je voudrais que tu m'*aimes*.	I would like you to love me.
Il faut que vous *finissiez* vos lettres ce soir.	You must finish your letters tonight.
On ira dans ta voiture, à moins que tu ne la *vendes*.	We'll go in your car, unless you sell it.

Past Subjunctive

The past subjunctive is formed with the present subjunctive of *avoir* or *être* and the past participle of the verb.

parler, finir, vendre

que j'*aie* parlé (fini/vendu)
que tu *aies* parlé (fini/vendu)
qu'il (elle, on) *ait* parlé
(fini/vendu)

que nous *ayons* parlé (fini/vendu)
que vous *ayez* parlé (fini/vendu)
qu'ils (elles) *aient* parlé (fini/vendu)

monter

que je *sois* monté(e)
que tu *sois* monté(e)
qu'il (elle, on) *soit* monté(e)

que nous *soyons* monté(e)s
que vous *soyez* monté(e)(s)
qu'ils (elles) *soient* monté(e)a

Je suis heureux que vous *ayez* aimé cette pièce.	I am happy that you liked that play.
C'est dommage qu'elle *soit* déjà partie.	It's a pity that she has already left.
Elle regrette que nous *ne soyons* pas venus.	She is sorry that we did not come.

Imperfect Subjunctive

The imperfect and the pluperfect of the subjunctive exist in classical literature. However, because of their cumbersome aspect, they are never used in spoken language. In modern literature, writers may still use the third person singular. Most of the time, however, the imperfect is replaced by the present subjunctive, and the pluperfect is replaced by the past subjunctive.

The imperfect subjunctive is formed with the *passé simple*. Drop the last letter of the first person singular and add the endings *-sse, -sses, - ^t, -ssions, -ssiez, -ssent*. These endings are the same for all verbs.

parler   finir

que je parla*sse*   que nous parla*ssions*   que je fini*sse*   que nous fini*ssions*
que tu parla*sses*   que vous parla*ssiez*   que tu fini*sses*   que vous fini*ssiez*
qu'il (elle, on)   qu'ils (elles)   qu'il (elle, on)   qu'ils (elles)
   parl*ât*   parla*ssent*   fin*ît*   fini*ssent*

vendre

que je vendi*sse*
que tu vendi*sses*
qu'il (elle, on) vend*ît*

que nous vendi*ssions*
que vous vendi*ssiez*
qu'ils (elles) vendi*ssent*

Il fallait qu'il vous *aimât* (aime) beaucoup pour faire cela.	He had to love you very much to do that.
Elle parlait fort pour qu'on *n'entendît* (entende) pas les cris de l'enfant.	She spoke loudly so that one could not hear the child crying.
Il insista pour que Marc *vendît* (vende) sa voiture.	He insisted that Marc sell his car.

Pluperfect Subjunctive

The pluperfect subjunctive is formed with the imperfect subjunctive of the auxiliary verbs *être* or *avoir* and the past participle.

parler, finir, vendre

que j'*eusse* parlé (fini/vendu)
que tu *eusses* parlé (fini/vendu)
qu'il (elle, on) *eût* parlé
  (fini/vendu)

que nous *eussions* parlé (fini/vendu)
que vous *eussiez* parlé (fini/vendu)
qu'ils (elles) *eussent* parlé
  (fini/vendu)

descendre

que je *fusse* descendu(e)
que tu *fusses* descendu(e)
qu'il (elle, on) *fût* descendu(e)

que nous *fussions* descendu(e)s
que vous *fussiez* descendu(e)(s)
qu'ils (elles) *fussent* descendu(e)s

**Serait-il possible qu'il l'*eût*
(ait) aimée plus que toutes les
autres?**

Would it be possible that he had
loved her more than all the
others?

**Nous n'avons pas pensé qu'il *fût*
(soit) déjà arrivé.**

We did not think that he had
already arrived.

Subjunctive Tenses

	-er		-ir		-re	
Present	___e	___ions	___isse	___issions	___e	___ions
	___es	___iez	___isses	___issiez	___es	___iez
	___e	___ent	___isse	___issent	___e	___ent
Past	aie ___é	ayons ___é	aie ___i	ayons ___i	aie ___u	ayons ___u
	aies ___é	ayez ___é	aies ___i	ayez ___i	aies ___u	ayez ___u
	ait ___é	aient ___é	ait ___i	aient ___i	ait ___u	aient ___u
	sois ___é	soyons ___é	sois ___i	soyons ___i	sois ___u	soyons ___u
	sois ___é	soyez ___é	sois ___i	soyez ___i	sois ___u	soyez ___u
	soit ___é	soient ___é	soit ___i	soient ___i	soit ___u	soient ___u
Imperfect	___asse	___assions	___isse	___issions	___isse	___issions
	___asses	___assiez	___isses	___issiez	___isses	___issiez
	___ât	___assent	___ît	___issent	___ît	___issent
Pluperfect	eusse ___é	eussions ___é	eusse ___i	eussions ___i	eusse ___u	eussions ___u
	eusses ___é	eussiez ___é	eusses ___i	eussiez ___i	eusses ___u	eussiez ___u
	eût ___é	eussent ___é	eût ___i	eussent ___i	eût ___u	eussent ___u
	fusse ___é	fussions ___é	fusse ___i	fussions ___i	fusse ___u	fussions ___u
	fusses ___é	fussiez ___é	fusses ___i	fussiez ___i	fusses ___u	fussiez ___u
	fût ___é	fussent ___é	fût ___i	fussent ___i	fût ___u	fussent ___u

Verb Synopsis of Subjunctive Tenses

parler - il

Present	qu'il parle	he speaks
Past	qu'il ait parlé	he spoke
Imperfect	qu'il parlât	he spoke
Pluperfect	qu'il eût parlé	he had spoken

arriver - il

Present	qu'il arrive	he arrives
Past	qu'il soit arrivé	he arrived
Imperfect	qu'il arrivât	he arrived
Pluperfect	qu'il fût arrivé	he had arrived

6. Uses of the Subjunctive

Use of the Subjunctive in Main and Independent Clauses

In Commands

The subjunctive in the main clause or in an independent clause is used to express a command, a suggestion, a wish, or a regret. It is used most often in the third person.

Que personne ne sorte!	No one can go out!
Que Dieu vous entende!	May God hear you!
Ah! Qu'elle ne fût jamais partie!	If only she had never left!

In Fixed Expressions

The subjunctive is also used in some fixed expressions such as the following:

Vivent les vacances!	Hurray for vacations!
Dieu vous bénisse!	God bless you!
Sauve qui peut!	Every man for himself!
Advienne que pourra!	Come what may!
Ainsi soit-il!	So be it! Amen!
Honni soit qui mal y pense!	Evil be to him who evil thinks!

Use of the Subjunctive in Dependent Clauses

After Impersonal Expressions

1. Most impersonal expressions that convey the speaker's will, desire, or judgment are followed by the subjunctive. All impersonal expressions are followed by *que*. Below is a list of the most common impersonal expressions requiring the subjunctive.

il faut	it is necessary	**il est préférable**	it is preferable
il est bon	it is good	**il est peu probable**	it is hardly probable
il est mauvais	it is bad	**il arrive**	it happens
il est bien	it is well	**il vaut mieux**	it is better
il est possible	it is possible	**il suffit**	it is sufficient
il semble	it seems	**c'est dommage**	it is a pity
il est important	it is important	**peu importe**	never mind
il est utile	it is useful	**nul doute**	no doubt
il est temps	it is time	**il se peut**	it may be
il est impossible	it is impossible		

Il arrive que nous soyons absents l'après-midi.	It happens that we are absent in the afternoon.
I faut que vous obéissiez à vos parents.	It is necessary for you to obey your parents.
Il se peut qu'ils aillent en France.	It may be that they are going to France.
Nul doute que tu aies l'intention de te marier.	No doubt you intend to marry.

2. Impersonal expressions that introduce a fact or certainty are followed by the indicative. Some of those expressions include:

il est certain	it is certain	il est probable	it is probable
il est évident	it is evident	il est vrai	it is true
il me semble	it seems to me	il paraît	it seems

Il est certain que l'hiver est arrivé.	It is certain that winter has come.
Il est évident que Paul ne reviendra pas.	It is evident that Paul will not come back.
Il est probable que nous avons trop mangé.	It is probable that we have eaten too much.

3. If the impersonal expressions indicating certainty are used in the negative in the main clause, the subjunctive is used in the dependent clause.

Il n'est pas vrai que les Français soient tous petits.	It is not true that the French are all short.
Il ne semble pas que vous ayez beaucoup travaillé.	It does not seem that you have worked much.

After Verbs of Volition

The subjunctive is used in dependent clauses after verbs expressing the speaker's mind or will: desire, judgment, command, or forbidding. The subjunctive is used in the dependent clause only when each clause has a different subject. If there is only one subject, an infinitive is used. Here is a partial list of verbs of volition:

aimer mieux } préférer }	to prefer	exiger	to demand, to require
souhaiter	to wish	tenir à ce (que)	to insist
permettre	to allow, to permit	vouloir	to want, to wish
conseiller	to advise	défendre	to forbid
ordonner	to command	demander	to ask
dire	to tell	prier	to pray, to beg
		compter	to expect

Ma mère me défend de sortir tard.	My mother forbids me to go out late.
Ma mère défend que nous sortions tard.	My mother forbids us to go out late.
J'exige que tu mettes de l'argent de côté.	I demand that you save money.
Ton père souhaite que tu n'oublies pas de lui écrire.	Your father wishes you not to forget to write him.
Elle veut que je fasse le ménage.	She wants me to do the housework.

After Verbs of Emotion

The subjunctive is also used after expressions of emotion (joy, fear, sorrow, regret, surprise).

avoir peur (...ne) to be afraid	**être surpris** to be surprised
être content to be glad, to be pleased	**se réjouir** to rejoice
être désolé to be sorry	**se plaindre** to complain
être enchanté to be delighted	**s'étonner** to be astonished
être heureux to be happy	**regretter** to regret
être malheureux to be unhappy	**craindre (...ne)** to fear

Je suis enchanté que vous ayez pu venir.	I am delighted that you could come.
Je m'étonne que vous travailliez si tard.	I am surprised that you are working so late.

NOTE: Some verbs, like *avoir peur* and *craindre,* call for *ne* in the subjunctive clause (without the effect of a negative), if the sentence is a declarative affirmative sentence. In negative and interrogative sentences the *ne* is omitted.

Craignez-vous qu'il soit malade?	Do you fear that he is sick?
Non, je crains qu'il *ne* mente.	No, I fear that he is lying.

After Verbs of Doubt and Denial

The subjunctive is also used after expressions of doubt and denial, when the speaker wants to convey the possibility of something in his mind, if not in reality.

douter to doubt	**croire** to believe, to think
ne pas être sûr to not be sure	**penser** to think
ne pas être certain to not be certain	**espérer** to hope

The verbs *croire, penser,* and *espérer* take the subjunctive only in negative and interrogative sentences.

Je ne suis pas sûre qu'elle ait pris son parapluie.	I am not sure that she has taken her umbrella.
Croyez-vous qu'elle soit malade?	Do you think she is sick?
Non, je crois qu'elle va bien.	No, I believe she is well.

After Conjunctions

The subjunctive is always used after the following conjunctions:

Time	Condition
avant que (...ne) before	**à moins que(...ne)** unless
en attendant que while waiting	**pourvu que** provided that, hopefully
jusqu'à ce que until	**sans que** without

Goal	Others
pour que in order that	**bien que** ⎫ although
afin que so that	**quoique** ⎭
de manière que ⎫ so that	**malgré que** despite the fact
de façon que ⎭	**puisque** since
	soit que...soit que either that...or that
Emotion	**qui que** whoever
de peur que (...ne) for fear that,	**quoi que** whatever
de crainte que (...ne) lest	

Qui que vous soyez, ouvrez la porte!	Whoever you are, open the door!
Nous irons à la plage, à moins qu'il ne pleuve.	We will go to the beach unless it rains.
Pourvu qu'il ne neige pas!	Hopefully, it will not snow!

In Relative Clauses

1. The subjunctive is used in a relative clause when the antecedent is a superlative or one of these adjectives: *seul, premier, dernier, unique, suprême*.

C'est la plus belle ville que j'aie jamais vue.	It is the most beautiful city I have ever seen.
C'est la seule langue que je connaisse.	It's the only language I know.

2. The subjunctive also comes after certain negatives: *rien, peu de, pas un, ne rien, ne personne.*

Je ne sais rien qui vaille la peine d'être répété.	I don't know anything that is worth repeating.
Il y a peu de chance qu'il réussisse.	There is little chance he will succeed.

3. When the sentence expresses a goal, an intention, or a consequence, the relative clause takes the subjunctive.

Je cherche quelqu'un qui parle chinois.	I am looking for someone who speaks Chinese.
Il n'y a personne qui puisse m'aider.	There is no one who could help me.

7. Orthographic-Changing Verbs

Orthographic-changing verbs are those verbs that change spelling in some forms in order to preserve a vowel or consonant sound.

1. Verbs whose infinitives end in -*cer* change the *c* to *ç* before *a* and *o* to retain the soft *c* sound.

commencer to begin, to start   *commençant*   *commencé* (aux. *avoir*)

    Pres. je commence, tu commences, il commence, **nous commençons,** vous commencez, ils commencent

    Imper. **je commençais, tu commençais, il commençait,** nous commencions, vous commenciez, **ils commençaient**

    Passé Simple **je commençai, tu commenças, il commença, nous commençâmes, vous commençâtes,** ils commencèrent

Other verbs of this type:

annoncer to announce	**menacer** to threaten
avancer to advance, to be fast (a watch)	**placer** to place, to set
	prononcer to pronounce
effacer to erase	**remplacer** to replace
exercer to exercise	**renoncer à** to give up
lancer to throw	

2. Verbs whose infinitives end in -*ger* add an *e* after *g* before *a* or *o* to retain the soft *g* sound.

manger to eat   *mangeant*   *mangé* (aux. *avoir*)

    Pres. je mange, tu manges, il mange, **nous mangeons,** vous mangez, ils mangent

    Imper. **je mangeais, tu mangeais, il mangeait,** nous mangions, vous mangiez, **ils mangeaient**

    Passé Simple **je mangeai, tu mangeas, il mangea, nous mangeâmes, vous mangeâtes,** ils mangèrent

Other verbs of this type:

arranger to put in order	**neiger** to snow
bouger to move	**obliger** to oblige
changer to change	**partager** to share
corriger to correct	**plonger** to dive, to plunge
déranger to disturb	**protéger** to protect
exiger to require	**songer** to imagine
infliger to inflict	**soulager** to ease (pain)
nager to swim	**voyager** to travel

3.   Verbs with infinitives ending in *-yer* change the *y* to an *i* before a mute *e*.

employer to use, to employ   *employant*   *employé* (aux. *avoir*)

   Pres.   **j'emploie, tu emploies, il emploie,** nous employons, vous employez, **ils emploient**
   Fut.   **j'emploierai, tu emploieras, il emploiera, nous emploierons, vous emploierez, ils emploieront**
   Cond.   **j'emploierais, tu emploierais, il emploierait, nous emploierions, vous emploieriez, ils emploieraient**

NOTE: Verbs ending in *-ayer* may keep the *y* or change to *i*: *il paye* or *il paie*.

Other verbs of this type:

balayer	to sweep	**nettoyer**	to clean
ennuyer	to bore	**se noyer**	to drown
essayer	to try	**payer**	to pay
essuyer	to wipe		

4. Verbs containing a mute *e* in the last syllable before the infinitive ending change the mute *e* to an *è* if the next syllable contains a mute *e*.

acheter to buy   *achetant*   *acheté* (aux. *avoir*)

   Pres.   **j'achète, tu achètes, il achète,** nous achetons, vous achetez, **ils achètent**
   Fut.   **j'achèterai, tu achèteras, il achètera, nous achèterons, vous achèterez, ils achèteront**
   Cond.   **j'achèterais, tu achèterais, il achèterait, nous achèterions, vous achèteriez, ils achèteraient**

Other verbs of this type:

achever	to complete	**se lever**	to get up
élever	to raise, to bring up	**mener**	to lead (someone)
emmener	to take away (someone)	**peser**	to weigh
lever	to raise	**se promener**	to take a walk

5.   Verbs with infinitives ending in *-eler* and *-eter* double the *l* or *t*.

jeter to throw (away)   *jetant*   *jeté* (aux. *avoir*)

   Pres.   **je jette, tu jettes, il jette,** nous jetons, vous jetez, **ils jettent**
   Fut.   **je jetterai, tu jetteras, il jettera, nous jetterons, vous jetterez, ils jetteront**
   Cond.   **je jetterais, tu jetterais, il jetterait, nous jetterions, vous jetteriez, ils jetteraient**

Other verbs of this type:

appeler	to call	**rappeler**	to call again
s'appeler	to be named	**se rappeler**	to recall

6.   Verbs with *é* in the next to last syllable of the infinitive change the *é* to *è* if the *e* is the last pronounced vowel.

préférer to prefer   *préférant*   *préféré* (aux. *avoir*)

   Pres.   **je préfère, tu préfères, il préfère,** nous préférons, vous préférez, **ils préfèrent**

Other verbs of this type:

céder to yield	**interpréter** to interpret
célébrer to celebrate	**posséder** to possess
compléter to complete	**protéger** to protect
espérer to hope	**répéter** to repeat
exagérer to exaggerate	**révéler** to reveal

NOTE: The verb *créer* ("to create") retains the *é* in all forms.

8. Irregular Verbs

In this chapter, only the irregular tenses are given; you may assume that the remaining tenses of the verbs are regular. Check regular tense formation in Chapter 2 (simple tenses), Chapter 3 (perfect tenses), and Chapter 5 (subjunctive mood). Present and past participles are given.

Auxiliary Verbs

avoir to have *ayant* *eu* (aux. *avoir*)

 Pres. j'ai, tu as, il a, nous avons, vous avez, ils ont
 Fut. j'aurai, tu auras, il aura, nous aurons, vous aurez, ils auront
 Pres. Subj. j'aie, tu aies, il ait, nous ayons, vous ayez, ils aient
 Passé Simple j'eus, tu eus, il eut, nous eûmes, vous eûtes, ils eurent
 Imperative aie, ayons, ayez

être to be *étant* *été* (aux. *avoir*)

 Pres. je suis, tu es, il est, nous sommes, vous êtes, ils sont
 Imper. j'étais, tu étais, il était, nous étions, vous étiez, ils étaient
 Fut. je serai, tu seras, il sera, nous serons, vous serez, ils seront
 Pres. Subj. je sois, tu sois, il soit, nous soyons, vous soyez, ils soient
 Passé Simple je fus, tu fus, il fut, nous fûmes, vous fûtes, il furent
 Imperative sois, soyons, soyez

Other Irregular Verbs

absoudre to absolve, to forgive *absolvant* *absous* (aux. *avoir*)

 Pres. j'absous, tu absous, il absout, nous absolvons, vous absolvez, ils absolvent

Other verbs of this type:

dissoudre to dissolve

acquérir to acquire *acquérant* *acquis* (aux. *avoir*)

 Pres. j'acquiers, tu acquiers, il acquiert, nous acquérons, vous acquérez, ils acquièrent
 Fut. j'acquerrai, tu acquerras, il acquerra, nous acquerrons, vous acquerrez, ils acquerront
 Passé Simple j'acquis, tu acquis, il acquit, nous acquîmes, vous acquîtes, ils acquirent

Other verbs of this type:

conquérir to conquer
requérir to ask for

aller to go   *allant*   *allé* (aux. *être*)

Pres. **je vais, tu vas, il va, nous allons, vous allez, ils vont**
Fut.   **j'irai, tu iras, il ira, nous irons, vous irez, ils iront**
Pres. Subj.   **j'aille, tu ailles, il aille, nous allions, vous alliez, ils aillent**

Other verbs of this type:

s'en aller to go away   (aux. *être*)

assaillir to assail   *assaillant*   *assailli* (aux. *avoir*)

Pres. **j'assaille, tu assailles, il assaille, nous assaillons, vous assaillez, ils assaillent**

Other verbs of this type:

défaillir to become feeble

asseoir to seat   *asseyant*   *assis* (aux. *avoir*)

Pres. **j'assieds, tu assieds, il assied, nous asseyons, vous asseyez, ils asseyent**
Fut.   **j'assiérai, tu assiéras, il assiéra, nous assiérons, vous assiérez, ils assiéront**
Passé Simple **j'assis, tu assis, il assit, nous assîmes, vous assîtes, ils assirent**

Other verbs of this type:

s'asseoir to sit down   (aux. *être*)
(se rasseoir to sit down again)

battre to beat   *battant*   *battu* (aux. *avoir*)

Pres. **je bats, tu bats, il bat, nous battons, vous battez, ils battent**

Other verbs of this type:

abattre   to knock down   **débattre**   to debate
combattre   to battle with   **se battre**   to fight

boire to drink   *buvant*   *bu* (aux. *avoir*)

Pres. **je bois, tu bois, il boit, nous buvons, vous buvez, ils boivent**
Passé Simple **je bus, tu bus, il but, nous bûmes, vous bûtes, ils burent**

bouillir to boil   *bouillant*   *bouilli* (aux. *avoir*)

Pres. **je bous, tu bous, il bout, nous bouillons, vous bouillez, ils bouillent**

conclure to conclude   *concluant*   *conclu* (aux. *avoir*)

Pres. **je conclus, tu conclus, il conclut, nous concluons, vous concluez, ils concluent**
Passé Simple **je conclus, tu conclus, il conclut, nous conclûmes, vous conclûtes, ils conclurent**

Other verbs of this type:

exclure to exclude
inclure to include

conduire to drive   *conduisant*   *conduit* (aux. *avoir*)

Pres. **je conduis, tu conduis, il conduit, nous conduisons, vous conduisez, ils conduisent**
Passé Simple **je conduisis, tu conduisis, il conduisit, nous conduisîmes, vous conduisîtes, ils conduisirent**

Other verbs of this type:

construire to build	**luire** to light up
cuire to cook	**nuire** to be hurtful
déduire to deduct	**produire** to produce
détruire to destruct	**réduire** to reduce
instruire to instruct	**reproduire** to reproduce
introduire to introduce	**traduire** to translate

connaître to know   *connaissant*   *connu* (aux. *avoir*)

Pres. **je connais, tu connais, il connaît, nous connaissons, vous connaissez, ils connaissent**
Passé Simple **je connus, tu connus, il connut, nous connûmes, vous connûtes, ils connurent**

Other verbs of this type:

apparaître to appear	**paraître** to seem, to appear
disparaître to disappear	**reconnaître** to recognize

coudre to sew   *cousant*   *cousu* (aux. *avoir*)

Pres. **je couds, tu couds, il coud, nous cousons, vous cousez, ils cousent**

courir to run   *courant*   *couru* (aux. *avoir*)

Pres. **je cours, tu cours, il court, nous courons, vous courez, ils courent**
Fut. **je courrai, tu courras, il courra, nous courrons, vous courrez, ils courront**

Other verbs of this type:

accourir to come running	**parcourir** to travel through
concourir to compete	**recourir** to resort
discourir to discourse	**secourir** to help, to come to
encourir to incur	the help of

craindre to fear   *craignant*   *craint* (aux. *avoir*)

Pres. **je crains, tu crains, il craint, nous craignons, vous craignez, ils craignent**
Passé Simple **je craignis, tu craignis, il craignit, nous craignîmes, vous craignîtes, ils craignirent**

Other verbs of this type:

atteindre to attain	**feindre** to feign, to simulate
dépeindre to depict	**joindre** to join
enceindre to surround	**peindre** to paint
enfeindre to infringe	**restreindre** to restrain
éteindre to extinguish	**teindre** to dye
étreindre to embrace	

croire to believe   *croyant*   *cru* (aux. *avoir*)

Pres. **je crois, tu crois, il croit, nous croyons, vous croyez, ils croient**
Passé Simple **je crus, tu crus, il crut, nous crûmes, vous crûtes, ils crurent**

croître to grow   *croissant*   *crû* (aux. *avoir*)

Pres. **je crois, tu crois, il croît, nous croissons, vous croissez, ils croissent**
Passé Simple **je crûs, tu crûs, il crût, nous crûmes, vous crûtes, ils crûrent**

Other verbs of this type:

accroître to increase
décroître to decrease

cueillir to pick (fruits and flowers)   *cueillant*   *cueilli* (aux. *avoir*)

Pres. **je cueille, tu cueilles, il cueille, nous cueillons, vous cueillez, ils cueillent**
Fut. **je cueillerai, tu cueilleras, il cueillera, nous cueillerons, vous cueillerez, ils cueilleront**

Other verbs of this type:

accueillir to welcome
recueillir to gather
se recueillir to collect one's thoughts

devoir must, to have to, should, to owe   *devant*   *dû* (aux. *avoir*)

Pres. **je dois, tu dois, il doit, nous devons, vous devez, ils doivent**
Pres. Subj. **je doive, tu doives, il doive, nous devions, vous deviez, ils doivent**
Passé Simple **je dus, tu dus, il dut, nous dûmes, vous dûtes, ils durent**

dire to say, to tell   *disant*   *dit* (aux. *avoir*)

Pres. **je dis, tu dis, il dit, nous disons, vous dites, ils disent**

Other verbs of this type:

contredire to contradict   **médire** to speak ill of
interdire to forbid   **prédire** to predict
maudire to curse

These have the ending *-isez* in the second person plural, except for *maudire,* with endings *-issons* and *-issez* in the first and second persons plural.

dormir to sleep   *dormant*   *dormi* (aux. *avoir*)

Pres. **je dors, tu dors, il dort, nous dormons, vous dormez, ils dorment**

Other verbs of this type:

endormir to put to sleep   **rendormir** to put back to sleep
s'endormir to go to sleep   **se rendormir** to go back to sleep

écrire to write   *écrivant*   *écrit* (aux. *avoir*)

Pres. **j'écris, tu écris, il écrit, nous écrivons, vous écrivez, ils écrivent**
Passé Simple **j'écrivis, tu écrivis, il écrivit, nous écrivîmes, vous écrivîtes, ils écrivirent**

Other verbs of this type:

décrire to describe   **souscrire** to subscribe
s'inscrire to register   **transcrire** to transcribe

envoyer to send   *envoyant*   *envoyé* (aux. *avoir*)

(See also Orthographic-Changing Verbs.)

Fut. **j'enverrai, tu enverras, il enverra, nous enverrons, vous enverrez, ils enverront**

Other verbs of this type:

renvoyer to send back, to fire (someone)

faillir to nearly do (something), to fail   *faillant*   *failli* (aux. *avoir)*

This verb is used only in the infinitive, passé simple, future, conditional, and perfect tenses.

Fut.   **je faillirai, tu failliras, il faillira, nous faillirons, vous faillirez, ils failliront**
Passé Simple   **je faillis, tu faillis, il faillit, nous faillîmes, vous faillîtes, ils faillirent**

faire to do, to make   *faisant*   *fait* (aux. *avoir)*

Pres.   **je fais, tu fais, il fait, nous faisons, vous faites, ils font**
Fut.   **je ferai, tu feras, il fera, nous ferons, vous ferez, ils feront**
Passé Simple   **je fis, tu fis, il fit, nous fîmes, vous fîtes, ils firent**

Other verbs of this type:

contrefaire to counterfeit	**refaire** to redo
défaire to undo	**satisfaire** to satisfy
parfaire to perfect	**surfaire** to overestimate

fuir to flee   *fuyant*   *fui* (aux. *avoir)*

Pres.   **je fuis, tu fuis, il fuit, nous fuyons, vous fuyez, ils fuient**

Other verbs of this type:

s'enfuir to flee

lire to read   *lisant*   *lu* (aux. *avoir)*

Pres.   **je lis, tu lis, il lit, nous lisons, vous lisez, ils lisent**
Passé Simple   **je lus, tu lus, il lut, nous lûmes, vous lûtes, ils lurent**

Other verbs of this type:

élire to elect	**relire** to reread
réélire to reelect	

mettre to put   *mettant*   *mis* (aux. *avoir)*

Pres.   **je mets, tu mets, il met, nous mettons, vous mettez, ils mettent**

Other verbs of this type:

admettre to admit	**permettre** to permit
commettre to commit	**remettre** to postpone
compromettre to compromise	**soumettre** to submit
émettre to emit	**transmettre** to transmit
omettre to omit	

moudre to grind   *moulant*   *moulu* (aux. *avoir)*

Pres.   **je mouds, tu mouds, il moud, nous moulons, vous moulez, ils moulent**
Passé Simple   **je moulus, tu moulus, il moulut, nous moulûmes, vous moulûtes, ils moulurent**

Other verbs of this type:

émoudre to sharpen

mourir to die   *mourant*   *mort* (aux. *être)*

Pres. **je meurs, tu meurs, il meurt, nous mourons, vous mourez, ils meurent**
Fut. **je mourrai, tu mourras, il mourra, nous mourrons, vous mourrez, ils mourront**
Passé Simple **je mourus, tu mourus, il mourut, nous mourûmes, vous mourûtes, il moururent**

mouvoir to move *mouvant* *mu* (aux. *avoir*)

Pres. **je meus, tu meus, il meut, nous mouvons, vous mouvez, ils meuvent**
Passé Simple **je mus, tu mus, il mut, nous mûmes, vous mûtes, ils murent**

Other verbs of this type:

émouvoir to move, to touch
s'émouvoir to be moved
promouvoir to promote

naître to be born *naissant* *né* (aux. *être*)

Pres. **je nais, tu nais, il naît, nous naissons, vous naissez, jls naissent**
Passé Simple **je naquis, tu naquis, il naquit, nous naquîmes, vous naquîtes, ils naquirent**

ouvrir to open *ouvrant* *ouvert* (aux. *avoir*)

Pres. **j'ouvre, tu ouvres, il ouvre, nous ouvrons, vous ouvrez, ils ouvrent**
Passé Simple **j'ouvris, tu ouvris, il ouvrit, nous ouvrîmes, vous ouvrîtes, ils ouvrirent**

Other verbs of this type:

couvrir to cover   **recouvrir** to recover
découvrir to discover   **rouvrir** to reopen
offrir to offer   **souffrir** to suffer

partir to leave *partant* *parti* (aux. *être*)

Pres. **je pars, tu pars, il part, nous partons, vous partez, ils partent**

Other verbs of this type:

départir to assign, to accord   **repartir** to leave again
se départir to abandon   **répartir** to distribute

plaire to please *plaisant* *plu* (aux. *avoir*)

Pres. **je plais, tu plais, il plaît, nous plaisons, vous plaisez, ils plaisent**
Passé Simple **je plus, tu plus, il plut, nous plûmes, vous plûtes, ils plurent**

Other verbs of this type:

déplaire to displease

pourvoir to provide *pourvoyant* *pourvu* (aux. *avoir*)

Pres. **je pourvois, tu pourvois, il pourvoit, nous pourvoyons, vous pourvoyez, ils pourvoient**
Fut. **je pourvoirai, tu pourvoiras, il pourvoira, nous pourvoirons, vous pourvoirez, ils pourvoiront**

pouvoir to be able to, can, may   *pouvant*   *pu* (aux. *avoir*)

Pres. **je peux, tu peux, il peut, nous pouvons, vous pouvez, il peuvent**
Fut. **je pourrai, tu pourras, il pourra, nous pourrons, vous pourrez, ils pourront**
Pres. Subj. **je puisse, tu puisses, il puisse, nous puissions, vous puissiez, ils puissent**

prendre to take   *prenant*   *pris* (aux. *avoir*)

Pres. **je prends, tu prends, il prend, nous prenons, vous prenez, ils prennent**
Pres. Subj. **je prenne, tu prennes, il prenne, nous prenions, vous preniez, ils prennent**
Passé Simple **je pris, tu pris, il prit, nous prîmes, vous prîtes, ils prirent**

Other verbs of this type:

apprendre to learn	**se méprendre** to be mistaken
comprendre to understand	**reprendre** to take back
entreprendre to undertake	**surprendre** to surprise

résoudre to resolve, to determine   *résolvant* *résolu* (determined) (aux. *avoir*)
                                            résous (resolved)

Pres. **je résous, tu résous, il résout, nous résolvons, vous résolvez, ils résolvent**
Passé Simple **je résolus, tu résolus, il résolut, nous résolûmes, vous résolûtes, ils résolurent**

rire to laugh   *riant*   *ri* (aux. *avoir*)

Pres. **je ris, tu ris, il rit, nous rions, vous riez, ils rient**

Other verbs of this type:

se rire de to laugh at
sourire to smile

savoir to know, to know how   *sachant*   *su* (aux. *avoir*)

Pres. **je sais, tu sais, il sait, nous savons, vous savez, ils savent**
Fut. **je saurai, tu sauras, il saura, nous saurons, vous saurez, ils sauront**
Pres. Subj. **je sache, tu saches, il sache, nous sachions, vous sachiez, ils sachent**
Imperative **sache, sachons, sachez**

sentir to feel, to smell   *sentant*   *senti* (aux. *avoir*)

Pres. **je sens, tu sens, il sent, nous sentons, vous sentez, ils sentent**

Other verbs of this type:

consentir to consent	**ressentir** to feel pain, emotion
démentir to deny	**se sentir** to feel
mentir to lie	**se repentir** to repent, rue

servir to serve   *servant*   *servi* (aux. *avoir*)

Pres. **je sers, tu sers, il sert, nous servons, vous servez, ils servent**

Other verbs of this type:

se servir de to use, to make use of

sortir to go out   *sortant*   *sorti* (aux. *être*)

Pres. **je sors, tu sors, il sort, nous sortons, vous sortez, ils sortent** *suffire* to suffice, to be sufficient   *suffisant*   *suffi* (aux. *avoir*)

Pres. **je suffis, tu suffis, il suffit, nous suffisons, vous suffisez, ils suffisent**

Other verbs of this type:

se suffire to be self-sufficient

suivre to follow   *suivant*   *suivi* (aux. *avoir*)

Pres. **je suis, tu suis, il suit, nous suivons, vous suivez, ils suivent**

Other verbs of this type:

poursuivre to pursue

taire to say nothing   *taisant*   *tu* (aux. *avoir*)

Pres. **je tais, tu tais, il tait, nous taisons, vous taisez, ils taisent**
Passé Simple **je tus, tu tus, il tut, nous tûmes, vous tûtes, ils turent**

Other verbs of this type:

se taire to be quiet, to hold one's tongue

traire to milk (a cow)   *trayant*   *trait* (aux. *avoir*)

Pres. **je trais, tu trais, il trait, nous trayons, vous trayez, ils traient**

This verb has no *passé simple* or imperfect subjunctive forms.

Other verbs of this type:

abstraire to abstract	**extraire** to extract
distraire to distract	**soustraire** to subtract

vaincre to conquer   *vainquant*   *vaincu* (aux. *avoir*)

Pres. **je vaincs, tu vaincs, il vainc, nous vainquons, vous vainquez, ils vainquent**
Passé Simple **je vainquis, tu vainquis, il vainquit, nous vainquîmes, vous vainquîtes, ils vainquirent**

Other verbs of this type:

convaincre to convince
se convaincre to convince oneself

valoir to be worth   *valant*   *valu* (aux. *avoir*)

Pres. **je vaux, tu vaux, il vaut, nous valons, vous valez, ils valent**
Fut. **je vaudrai, tu vaudras, il vaudra, nous vaudrons, vous vaudrez, ils vaudront**
Pres. Subj. **je vaille, tu vailles, il vaille, nous valions, vous valiez, ils vaillent**

venir to come   *venant*   *venu* (aux. *être*)

Pres. **je viens, tu viens, il vient, nous venons, vous venez, ils viennent**
Fut. **je viendrai, tu viendras, il viendra, nous viendrons, vous viendrez, ils viendront**
Passé Simple **je vins, tu vins, il vint, nous vînmes, vous vîntes, ils vinrent**

Other verbs of this type:
(with *avoir* as the auxiliary)

appartenir à to belong to	**prévenir** to warn
contenir to contain	**retenir** to hold back
convenir à to suit, to be suitable	**soutenir** to support
détenir to hold, to detain	**subvenir** to provide for
intervenir to intervene	**survenir** to happen unexpectedly
maintenir to maintain	**tenir** to hold
obtenir to obtain	

(with *être* as the auxiliary)

se convenir to agree with each other	**revenir** to come back
devenir to become	**se souvenir de** to remember
parvenir to attain, succeed (in)	**se tenir** to remain, to keep

vêtir to clothe   *vêtant*   *vêtu* (aux. *avoir*)

Pres.   **je vêts, tu vêts, il vêt, nous vêtons, vous vêtez, ils vêtent**
Passé Simple   **je vêtis, tu vêtis, il vêtit, nous vêtîmes, vous vêtîtes, ils vêtirent**

Other verbs of this type:

se vêtir   to clothe oneself

vivre to live   *vivant*   *vécu* (aux. *avoir*)

Pres.   **je vis, tu vis, il vit, nous vivons, vous vivez, ils vivent**
Passé Simple   **je vécus, tu vécus, il vécut, nous vécûmes, vous vécûtes, ils vécurent**

Other verbs of this type:

survivre   to survive

voir to see   *voyant*   *vu* (aux. *avoir*)

Pres.   **je vois, tu vois, il voit, nous voyons, vous voyez, ils voient**
Fut.   **je verrai, tu verras, il verra, nous verrons, vous verrez, ils verront**
Passé Simple   **je vis, tu vis, il vit, nous vîmes, vous vîtes, ils virent**

Other verbs of this type:

apercevoir to have a glimpse of	**prévoir** to foresee (Fut.:
s'apercevoir to realize	*je prévoirai*, etc.)

vouloir to want, to wish   *voulant*   *voulu* (aux. *avoir*)

Pres.   **je veux, tu veux, il veut, nous voulons, vous voulez, ils veulent**
Fut.   **je voudrai, tu voudras, il voudra, nous voudrons, vous voudrez, ils voudront**
Pres. Subj.   **je veuille, tu veuilles, il veuille, nous voulions, vous vouliez, ils veuillent**
Imperative   **veuille, veuillons, veuillez**

Other verbs of this type:

en vouloir à   to bear ill will

9. Impersonal Verbs

Impersonal verbs are those that are used only in the third person singular with no definite subject.

Il y a

The expression *il y a* ("there is," "there are") implies existence. *Il y a* is used in any tense.

Il y a des fleurs sur la table.	There are flowers on the table.
Hier, il y avait beaucoup de fruits dans le jardin.	Yesterday, there was a lot of fruit in the garden.
C'est dommage qu'il y ait tant de monde.	It's too bad there are so many people.
Il n'y avait rien qui lui fasse peur.	There was nothing that frightened him.

Il y a is used in several common idiomatic expressions.

Qu'est-ce qu'il y a?	What's the matter?
Il y a quelque chose qui ne va pas.	There is something the matter.
Merci. Il n'y a pas de quoi.	Thank you. Don't mention it.
Il n'y a pas moyen d'être tranquille ici?	Could we have some quiet here?
Il y en a qui disent que la guerre va arriver.	There are some people who say that there will be a war.

Il y a is also used to express "ago," "for," and "since."

Je suis partie il y a un mois.	I left a month ago.
Il y a deux heures que je l'attends.	I have been waiting for him for two hours.
Il y a longtemps que je ne t'ai vu.	It's been a long time since I saw you.

Falloir

Falloir, "to be necessary," is one of the most commonly used impersonal verbs.

The forms of *falloir* most commonly used are: Present: **il faut**; Imperfect: **il fallait**; Passé Simple: **il fallut**; Future: **il faudra**; Conditional: **il faudrait**; Passé Composé: **il a fallu**; Pluperfect: **il avait fallu**; Future Perfect: **il aura fallu**; Past Conditional: **il aurait fallu**; Present Subjunctive: **il faille**.

Falloir is followed by the subjunctive or an infinitive.

Il faudrait que nous fassions la vaisselle.	It would be necessary for us to do the dishes.
Il a fallu qu'il prenne son billet un mois à l'avance.	He had to buy his ticket a month in advance.
Il faut manger pour vivre.	One must eat to live.
Il me faut des poireaux et des carottes pour la soupe.	I need leeks and carrots for the soup.

Idiomatic uses of *falloir:*

Mets le couvert comme il faut.	Set the table properly.
C'est plus qu'il n'en faut.	That's more than enough.
Voilà l'homme qu'il nous faut.	He's the very man we need.
Il s'en faut de beaucoup.	Not by a long shot.

Weather Expressions

bruiner	**il bruine**	it's drizzling
geler	**il gèle**	it's freezing

Two other verbs are conjugated like *geler: dégeler,* "to thaw," and *regeler,* "to freeze again." See Orthographic-Changing Verbs, Chapter 7.

grêler	**il grêle**	it's hailing

A verb conjugated like *grêler* is *regrêler,* "to hail again."

neiger	**il neige**	it's snowing

(See Orthographic-Changing Verbs, Chapter 7.) *Reneiger,* "to snow again," is conjugated like *neiger.*

pleuvoir	**il pleut**	it's raining

Other forms of *pleuvoir* are: Imperfect: **il pleuvait;** Passé Simple: **il plut;** Future: **il pleuvra;** Conditional: **il pleuvrait;** Past Participle: **plu;** Present Participle: **pleuvant;** Present Subjunctive: **il pleuve.** *Repleuvoir,* "to rain again," is conjugated like *pleuvoir.*

tonner	**il tonne**	it's thundering

Il ne cessa de bruiner.	It was drizzling constantly.
On gèle ici!	It's freezing here!
Il a grêlé pendant au moins un quart d'heure.	Hail fell for at least a quarter of an hour.
J'espère qu'il va neiger pour Noël.	I hope it snows at Christmas time.
Il pleut des cordes.	It's pouring.
Il a tonné pendant l'orage.	There was thunder during the storm.

Weather Expressions with *Faire*

Il fait beau.	The weather is beautiful.	**Il fait mauvais.**	The weather is bad.
Il fait chaud.	It's warm (hot).	**Il fait sombre.**	It's dark.
Il fait frais.	It's chilly.	**Il fait du brouillard.**	It's foggy.
Il fait froid.	It's cold.	**Il fait de la brume.**	It's hazy (misty).
Il fait lourd.	It's muggy.	**Il fait de l'orage.**	It's stormy.
Il fait du soleil.	It's sunny.	**Il fait du vent.**	It's windy.

NOTE: For more information on impersonal verbs and expressions, see Chapter 6, Uses of the Subjunctive.

10. Sequence of Tenses

The action expressed in a dependent clause can be simultaneous to, can precede, or can follow the action expressed in the main clause. This is true of sentences in the indicative mood, conditional sentences, and sentences calling for the subjunctive.

Tenses of the Indicative

Past Time					Present Time	Future Time	
	Imperfect						
Passé Simple		Passé Surcomposé					
Pluperfect	Preterite Perfect	Passé Composé	Future Perfect of the Past	Future of the Past	Present	Future Perfect	Future

The above chart shows a sequence of tenses in time. The tense most removed in past time is the pluperfect (*plus-que-parfait*); the farthest in the future is the future.

1. The *passé surcomposé* is formed by adding the *passé composé* of *être* or *avoir* to the past participle of the verb. It is mostly used after conjunctions of time: *quand, lorsque, dès que, aussitôt que.*

Dès qu'elle *a été aimée* **pour elle-même, elle a guéri.**	As soon as she was loved for herself, she was cured.
Quand j'*ai eu fini***, il a été convaincu.**	When I finished, he was convinced.

2. The future perfect of the past (*futur antérieur du passé*) has the same forms as the past conditional.

J'étais sûre qu'il *aurait oublié* **son parapluie.**	I was sure he would forget his umbrella.

3. The future of the past (*futur du passé*) indicates an action that follows a time in the past. It is formed the same way as the present conditional.

Il m'a dit qu'il *partirait* **à sept heures.**	He told me he would leave at seven o'clock.

Present Time

When the indicative present is used in the main clause, the choice of tense used in the dependent clause depends upon the time of its action in relation to the present — whether it is simultaneous to, precedes, or follows the action in the main clause. Or, as in the last two examples, the tense of the dependent clause may depend upon the time of another action.

Je *pense* qu'elle *part* maintenant.	I think she is leaving now.
Elle *dit* qu'elle *partira* à dix heures.	She says that she's going to leave at ten o'clock.
Il *dit* qu'elle *est partie* à sept heures.	He says that she left at seven o'clock.
Tu *sais* qu'elle *cherchait* une situation.	You know that she was looking for a job.
Nous *savons* qu'elle *avait déjà accepté* cette offre.	We know that she had already accepted this offer.

Past Time
Imparfait vs Passé Composé (or passé simple)

In order to understand when to use either the *imparfait* or the *passé composé* (or the *passé simple*), imagine that you are seeing a movie and that you want to describe its story line. When the frames, or actions, follow each other quickly on the screen, in a series of short scenes — separate actions which are over and done quickly — they should be described in either the *passé composé* or the *passé simple*. But when the cameraman lingers on a scene — a long scene with not much happening — the scene should be described in the *imparfait*.

Long scene:

Le soleil *se couchait* à l'horizon et le cavalier solitaire *s'éloignait* à toute allure dans sa direction.	The sun was setting on the horizon and the lone horseman was moving toward it at full speed.

Short, quick scenes:

Un groupe d'Indiens *est apparu* (or *apparut*) sur le haut de la colline.	A group of Indians appeared at the top of the hill.
Ils *ont regardé* (or *regardèrent*) le soleil couchant et *ont vu* (or *virent*) le cavalier.	They looked toward the sunset and saw the horseman.

Other Past Tenses

The tense used in the dependent clause is always one tense removed (back or ahead) from the past tense used in the main clause, unless the actions are simultaneous.

Je *savais* qu'elle *cherchait* une situation.	I knew she was looking for a job.
Je ne *savais* pas qu'elle *avait déjà accepté* cette offre.	I didn't know she had already accepted that offer.
Elle *a dit* qu'elle *partirait* à dix heures.	She said she would leave at ten o'clock.
Je ne *savais* pas qu'elle *était partie* à sept heures.	I did not know she had gone at seven o'clock.

Special Uses of the Imperfect

1. The imperfect (*imparfait*) must be used after a main clause using *dire, croire, demander, se demander, estimer,* or *penser* in the past.

Il *a pensé* qu'elle *voulait* l'embrasser.	He thought that she wanted to kiss him.

2. The imperfect functions as a present-in-the-past in dependent clauses starting with a relative pronoun (when the main clause is in the past).

J'*ai vu* un homme qui *portait* un chapeau.	I saw a man who was wearing a hat.
Nous *avons acheté* le piano dont je te *parlais*.	We bought the piano I told you about.

3. The imperfect also functions as a present-in-the-past in dependent clauses expressing time, cause or consequence.

Elle *déjeunait* au moment où vous *avez téléphoné*.	She was having lunch when you phoned.

Future Time

Here again, as with main clauses in the present, the choice of tense in the dependent clause depends upon the time of its action in relation to the future-time action of the main clause.

Elle *partira* quand elle *sera* prête.	She will leave when she is ready.
Donne mon cadeau à ta grand-mère quand tu *arriveras*.	Give my present to your grandmother when you arrive.
J'*irai* la voir puisque tu me l'*as demandé*.	I will go see her since you asked me.
Elle *sera rentrée* à midi.	She will be back at noon.

NOTE: In French the future is used after *quand, lorsque, dès que,* and *aussitôt que* when future time is implied.

Conditional Sentences

Note the sequence of actions in the following table and the corresponding examples given below.

Dependent Clause	Main Clause
1. *Si* plus the present indicative	(a) Present Indicative
	(b) Future
	(c) Future Perfect
	(d) Imperative
2. *Si* plus the passé composé	(a) Present Indicative
	(b) Future
	(c) Future Perfect
	(d) Imperfect
	(e) Passé Composé
	(f) Imperative
3. *Si* plus imperfect	(a) Conditional
	(b) Past Conditional
4. *Si* plus pluperfect	(a) Conditional
	(b) Past Conditional

1. Si je *sors* **maintenant, j'***emmène* **le chien.**	If I go out now, I am taking the dog.
Si tu *sors* **ce soir, tu** *emmèneras* **le chien.**	If you go out tonight, you'll take the dog.
Si elle *sort* **maintenant, elle** *sera* **rentrée dans une heure.**	If she goes out now, she'll be back in an hour.
Si vous *sortez,* **emmenez le chien.**	If you go out, take the dog.
2. Si tu *as* **bien** *appris* **tes leçons, tu ne** *peux* **pas les oublier.**	If you learned your lessons well, you can't forget them.
Si nous *avons fait* **nos devoirs, nous** *aurons* **une bonne note.**	If we have done our homework, we'll get a good grade.
Si vous *avez* **déjà** *fait* **cette tâche, vous** *aurez fini* **rapidement.**	If you have already done this task, you'll be finished quickly.
S'il ne t'*a* **pas** *saluée,* **c'est qu'il** *était* **distrait.**	If he did not greet you, it is because he was absent-minded
S'il ne vous *a* **pas** *appelé,* **c'est qu'il n'***a* **pas** *reçu* **votre lettre.**	If he has not called you, it must be that he has not received your letter.
Si nous ne *sommes* **pas** *rentrés* **à dix heures,** *appelez* **la police.**	If we have not come back by ten o'clock, call the police.
3. Si tu *voyais* **Venise, tu ne** *l'oublierais* **jamais.**	If you saw Venice, you'd never forget it.
Si tu *payais* **tes dettes regulièrement, tu ne** *serais* **jamais** *endettée.*	If you paid your debts regularly, you would never be in debt.
4. Si elles nous *avaient écrit,* **nous** *aurions* **des nouvelles de la famille.**	If they had written us, we would have news from the family.
Si vous *aviez eu* **du courage, vous n'***auriez* **pas** *refusé.*	If you had had the courage, you would not have refused.

Sentences Calling for the Subjunctive

In a dependent clause where the verb is in the subjunctive, the tense of the verb depends: (1) on the tense of the verb in the main clause and (2) on the relationship of the dependent clause with the main clause. In the following table, the tenses in italics are those used exclusively in literature.

Main Clause	Dependent Clause
1. Indicative Present or Future	Subjunctive Present or Past
2. Passé Composé	Subjunctive Present or Past
3. *Passé Simple,* Imperfect, or Pluperfect	Subjunctive *Imperfect* or *Pluperfect*
4. Present Conditional	Subjunctive Present or Past
5. Past Conditional	Subjunctive Present or Past; Subjunctive *Imperfect* or *Pluperfect*

1. **Nous** *sommes* **contents qu'il** *fasse* **beau.**
We are happy that the weather is nice

   Nous *serons* **contents que tu** *fasses* **ce voyage.**
We will be happy that you go on that trip.

   Je *suis* **heureux que vous** *ayez pu* **faire ce voyage.**
I am glad that you could take this trip.

   Il *ira* **dans les Alpes à moins qu'il** **n'***ait neigé.*
He will go to the Alps unless it has snowed.

2. **Il** *a fallu* **qu'il** *vienne* **au mauvais moment!**
He had to come at a bad time!

   Elle *a regretté* **que ça se** *soit passé* **comme ça.**
She was sorry that it had happened that way.

3. **Ils** *passèrent* **le col sans difficultés bien qu'il** *neigeât.*
They went through the pass even though it was snowing.

   Il *fallait* **qu'il** *fît* **ce voyage en janvier.**
He had to take that trip in January.

   On *était parti* **sans qu'elles nous** *eussent entendus.*
We had gone without their having heard us.

4. **Je** *voudrais* **que vous** *fassiez* **la vaisselle.**
I would like you to do the dishes.

   Il *faudrait* **que nous** *soyons arrivés* **à Naples la semaine prochaine.**
It is necessary that we arrive in Naples next week.

5. **Il** *aurait fallu* **que vous** *fassiez* **réparer la voiture avant de partir.**
It would have been necessary for you to have the car repaired before leaving.

   *Aurait-***il** *été* **possible qu'ils** *aient acheté* **la maison à ce moment-là?**
Would it have been possible for them to buy the house at that time?

   Nous *aurions préféré* **qu'il n'***eût* **rien** *dit.*
We would have preferred for him to have said nothing.

   Est-ce que tu *aurais préféré* **qu'ils** *fussent* **plus riches?**
Would you have preferred for them to have been richer?

11. Auxiliary Verbs

In addition to the auxiliary verbs *avoir* and *être*, which are used in the perfect tenses, there are other verbs that have a similar function before an infinitive. They may be auxiliary of time, of mode, or of aspect.

Aller + Infinitive

To express the immediate future (*le futur proche*) of the present, future, or past time (imperfect), one uses the verb *aller* followed by an infinitive. This construction is equivalent to "to be going to."

Je *vais* lui *répondre* tout de suite.	I am going to answer him right away.
Tu *allais* lui *répondre* hier, mais tu ne l'as pas fait.	You were going to answer him yesterday, but you did not do it.
Tu n'*iras* pas m'*accuser* de négligence!	You are not going to accuse me of negligence!

Venir de + Infinitive

To express the immediate past (*le passé immédiat*) of present, future, or past time (imperfect), one uses *venir de* before an infinitive. This is the equivalent of "to have just."

Ton père *vient de rentrer*.	Your father just came home.
Nous *venions d'arriver* quand vous avez téléphoné.	We had just arrived when you phoned.

Être en train de

To emphasize the duration of an action, one may use *être en train de* + infinitive. This expresses the idea of doing something or of being in the process of doing something.

Je *suis en train de travailler*.	I am working.
Elle *était en train de faire des confitures*.	She was making jam.

Devoir

Devoir has many meanings, depending on the tense in which it is used.

Ça *devrait* être bon.	It ought to be good.
Votre maison *doit* être belle.	Your house must be beautiful.
Je *dois* être au bureau à neuf heures et demie.	I have to be at the office at nine-thirty.

Être sur le point de

This verb expresses the sense of "to be about to," "to be on the verge of."

Il *était sur le point de* partir.	He was about to leave.

Être loin de

This verb is used to express the sense of being far from doing something or being far from being something.

Marc *est* **bien** *loin d'être* **bête.**	Marc is far from being stupid.

Ce n'est pas pour

This verb is always used in the negative.

Ce n'est pas pour **me déplaire.**	This is not displeasing to me.

Faillir

This verb is used to express the meaning of nearly doing something or for something to nearly happen.

Il *a* **bien** *failli mourir.*	He nearly died.

Laisser

This verb means to let someone do something or to let something happen.

Laissez-**le** *partir.*	Let him go.
Il faut *laisser faire* **les choses.**	One must let things go their way.

Paraître and Sembler

Le ciel *paraît changer* **de couleurs.**	The sky seems to change colors.
Il *semble comprendre.*	He seems to understand.

Pouvoir and Vouloir

Il *voulait partir* **mais ne** *pouvait* **pas** *se lever.*	He wanted to leave but could not get up.

12. The Present Participle

The present participle (*le participe présent*) is formed by replacing the *-ons* ending of the first person plural present of regular verbs with the ending *-ant*. The present participle can be used as a verbal form, an adjective, or as part of a clause.

Infinitive	Present Participle
aimer	aimant
finir	finissant
vendre	vendant

A few present participles are irregular: *sachant (savoir), étant (être), ayant (avoir)*. See Chapter 8, Irregular Verbs, for other irregular present participles.

1. The present participle is used as a verbal form to express an action simultaneous with the action of the main verb. It is invariable when used in this way.

C'est une jolie bague, *valant* plus de mille dollars.	It's a pretty ring, worth more than a thousand dollars.
Une secrétaire *parlant* plusieurs langues vaut son pesant d'or.	A secretary speaking several languages is worth her weight in gold.
Connaissant le problème, il hésita.	Knowing the problem, he hesitated.

2. Adjectives formed with present participles agree in gender and number with the nouns they modify.

Ils ont *l'eau courante* dans leur ferme.	They have running water in their farm.
C'est *une rue passante*.	It's a busy street.
Nous allons samedi à *une soirée dansante*.	We're going to a dancing party next Saturday.

3. The gerund is formed with a present participle and the preposition *en*. The gerund modifies a verbal clause to express (a) the manner, (b) the means, (c) the cause, or (d) the time at which the action of the main clause took place. The two actions are simultaneous.

(a) Il faisait la grimace *en mangeant* ses escargots.	He was making a face while eating his snails.
Elle est arrivée *en sifflotant*.	She arrived whistling lightly.
(b) Les enfants sont arrivés *en courant*.	The children came running.
En faisant un grand effort, il a réussi à sauter par-dessus la barrière.	Making a tremendous effort, he was able to jump over the fence.

(c) C'est *en forgeant* qu'on devient forgeron.

It is by forging that one becomes a blacksmith.

Il est arrivé à se faire une belle situation *en travaillant* dur.

He managed to get a nice job by working hard.

(d) *En attendant,* elle est bien malheureuse.

In the meantime, she is very unhappy.

En passant devant elle, il admira sa robe.

When he passed in front of her, he admired her dress.

13. Active and Passive Voices

In the active voice, the subject performs an action. In the passive voice, the subject receives the action or is acted upon.

Active:	**Le feu a détruit notre sapin de Noël.**	Fire destroyed our Christmas tree.
Passive:	**Notre sapin de Noël a été détruit par le feu.**	Our Christmas tree was destroyed by fire.

The passive construction is formed with any tense of the verb *être* and a past participle. The past participle always agrees in number and gender with the subject. It is followed by *par* if the action is physical and *de* if it is mental.

Tout le monde aimait Jean. (*active*)	Everybody liked Jean.
Jean est aimé de tout le monde. (*passive*)	Jean is liked by everyone.
Une vague a renversé notre bateau. (*active*)	A wave tipped over our boat.
Notre bateau a été renversé par une vague. (*passive*)	Our boat was tipped over by a wave.

NOTE: *On* is never used in the passive voice. Pronominal (reflexive) verbs cannot be used in the passive voice.

Conjugation of the Passive Voice

Simple Tenses		Perfect Tenses	
Present	**je suis aimé(e)**	Past Perfect	**j'ai été aimé(e)**
Imperfect	**j'étais aimé(e)**	Pluperfect	**j'avais été aimé(e)**
Future	**je serai aimé(e)**	Future Perfect	**j'aurai été aimé(e)**
Passé Simple	**je fus aimé(e)**	Preterite Perfect	**j'eus été aimé(e)**
Present Subjunctive	**je sois aimé(e)**	Past Subjunctive	**j'eusse été aimé(e)**
Present Conditional	**je serais aimé(e)**	Past Conditional	**j'aurais été aimé(e)**
Infinitive	**être aimé(e)**	Past Infinitive	**avoir été aimé(e)**
Present Participle	**étant aimé(e)**	Past Present Participle	**ayant été aimé(e)**

14. Verbs Followed by a Preposition

1. The following verbs require the preposition *à* when followed by an infinitive. The preposition is not always translated into English.

aider (quelqu'un) à	to help (someone) to	encourager (quelqu'un) à	to encourage (someone) to
s'amuser à	to amuse oneself (by)	forcer (quelqu'un)	to force (someone) to
apprendre à	to learn (how) to	s'habituer à	to get used to
avoir à	to have to	s'intéresser à	to be interested in
avoir de la peine à	to have difficulty (in)	inviter (quelqu'un) à	to invite (someone) to
commencer à	to begin (to)	réussir à	to succeed (in)
continuer à	to continue (to)		

Il est tellement malade qu'il *a de la peine à se lever.*	He is so sick that he has difficulty getting up.

2. The following verbs require the preposition *de* when followed by an infinitive.

s'arrêter de to stop	avoir de la chance de to be lucky to
cesser de to stop	avoir envie de to want to
choisir de to choose to	avoir hâte de to be in a hurry to
décider de to decide to	avoir le droit de to have the right to
se dépêcher de to hurry	avoir le temps de to have the time to
essayer de to try to	avoir peur de to be afraid of
finir de to finish	avoir raison de to be right to
oublier de to forget to	avoir tort de to be wrong to
refuser de to refuse to	en avoir assez de to have enough of

3. Some verbs can be followed by both *à* (followed by a person) and *de* (followed by the infinitive).

conseiller à (quelqu'un) de (faire quelque chose)	to advise (someone) to do something	offrir à...de	to offer (to someone) to
		permettre à...de	to allow (someone) to
défendre à...de	to forbid (someone) to	promettre à...de	to promise (someone) to
demander à...de	to ask (someone) to	proposer à...de	to propose (to someone) to
dire à...de	to tell (someone) to	suggérer à...de	to suggest (to someone) to

J'ai conseillé à ma fille *de partir en vacances.*	I advised my daughter to go on vacation.
Paul *a dit à* sa sœur *de* se taire.	Paul told his sister to shut up.

4. Some verbs can be followed directly by an infinitive.

aimer to love (to)	**espérer** to hope to
aimer bien to like (to)	**falloir** to be necessary
aimer mieux to prefer	**pouvoir** can, to be able to
aller to be going to	**préférer** to prefer
compter to intend to	**regarder** to look at
désirer to wish to	**savoir** to know how to
détester to detest	**souhaiter** to wish
devoir to have to, to be obligated to	**voir** to see
écouter to listen	**vouloir** to want, to wish
entendre to hear	

J'*aimerais mieux partir* **plus tard.**	I'd rather leave later.
Nous *savons faire* **du vélo.**	We know how to ride a bike.
Je l'*ai entendu tomber.*	I heard him fall.

5. The verb *compter* sometimes takes the prepositions *sur* and *pour*.

compter sur (quelqu'un) pour faire (quelque chose)

Je *compte sur* **toi** *pour* **préparer les hors d'œuvre.**	I am counting on you to prepare the hors d'œuvre.

Part Two:
Essentials of Grammar

15. Articles

	Singular	Plural	
Definite Article: *the*	le	les	*(m.)*
	la	les	*(f.)*
	l'	les	*(m. & f.)*
Indefinite Article: *a, an, some*	un	des	*(m.)*
	une	des	*(f.)*

The Definite Article

The definite article, *le, la, les,* agrees in number and gender with the noun. *L'* replaces *le* or *la* before a noun starting with a vowel or a mute *h*.

Singular	Plural
le livre the book	**les livres** the books
la carte the map	**les cartes** the maps

l'eau *(f.)* the water
l'air *(m.)* the air
l'étudiant *(m.)* the student (male)
l'étudiante *(f.)* the student (female)

Contractions:

The preposition *à* contracts with *le* and *les*. It does not contract with *la* or *l'*.

à + le = au
à + les = aux

Je parle *au* **facteur.**	I am speaking to the mailman.
Il parle *aux* **étudiants.**	He is speaking to the students.
Nous allons *à l'***université.**	We go to the university.
Ils rentrent *à la* **maison.**	They are going home.

The preposition *de* also contracts with *le* and *les*. It does not contract with *la* or *l'*.

de + le = du
de + les = des

Elle parle *du* **professeur.**	She is talking about the teacher.
Nous parlons *des* **étudiantes.**	We are talking about the students.
Elles parlent *de la* **voisine.**	They are talking about the neighbor.
Ils parlent *de l'***économie.**	They are talking about the economy.

Uses

The definite article is used with:

1. Nouns used in a general or abstract sense and collective nouns.

L'or **est précieux.**	Gold is precious.
Les enfants **sont en vacances.**	The children are on vacation.
La gourmandise **est un péché.**	Gluttony is a sin.
Les gens **sont malheureux.**	People are unhappy.

2. Adjectives and verbs used as nouns.

Elle préfère *le vert.*	She prefers green.
Le manger **et** *le boire.*	Food and drinks.

3. Names of languages.

Il ne parle que *l'anglais.*	He speaks only English.
Le français **est sa langue maternelle.**	French is his native tongue.

NOTE: The definite article is not used after the verb *parler,* after *en,* or after *de* (in an adjective phrase).

Ici, on parle *français.*	French is spoken here.
Combien de livres avez-vous lus *en français?*	How many books have you read in French?
J'ai perdu mon livre *de latin.*	I have lost my Latin book.

4. Titles of rank or profession.

le docteur **Freud**	Doctor Freud
le général **de Gaulle**	General de Gaulle
le président **de la République**	the President of the Republic

NOTE: The definite article is omitted in numerical titles of monarchs.

François Premier	François the First
Henri IV	Henry the Fourth

5. Geographical names.

La Corse **fait partie de** *la France.*	Corsica is part of France.
Le Rhône **se jette dans** *la mer Méditerranée.*	The Rhône river flows into the Mediterranean Sea.
Il va *au Canada.*	He is going to Canada.

NOTE: Names of cities, towns, and villages do not take an article, except those which are qualified by an adjective or a clause, and those that already have an article in their name *(La Nouvelle Orléans, Le Havre).*

J'adore *Paris.*	I love Paris.
Le vieux Québec.	Old Quebec.
Le Lyon que je connais.	The Lyon I know.

NOTE: The names of some islands do not take the article: *Madagascar, Tahiti, Haïti, Hawaï.*

6. Names of seasons.

Je déteste *l'hiver.*	I hate winter.
Nous reviendrons *au printemps.*	We will come back in the spring.

7. Units of measure.

Ces pommes coûtent cinq francs *la livre.*	These apples cost 5 F. a pound.
On achète ce matériel *au mètre.*	You buy this material by the meter.

8. Dates.

Nous sommes *le vingt-cinq décembre.*	It's the 25th of December.
Paris, *le 14 juillet 1983.*	Paris, July 14, 1983.

The Indefinite Article

The indefinite article, *un, une, des,* agrees in number and gender with the noun.

Singular	Plural
un livre a book	**des livres** (some) books
une carte a map	**des cartes** (some) maps
J'ai *un ami* **à Paris.**	I have a friend in Paris.
Tu vas prendre *des pommes frites?*	Are you going to have french fries?

In the negative, *un, une,* and *des* are replaced by *de.*

Tu as *une carte?*	Do you have a map?
Non, je *n'ai pas de* **carte.**	No, I don't have a map.

NOTE: For further information on the negative, see Chapter 24.

Omission of the Article

The definite and indefinite articles are omitted in the following circumstances:

1. After the exclamatory adjective *quel (quelle, quels, quelles).*

Quelle foule!	What a crowd!

2. Before the numbers *cent* and *mille.*

Tu me l'as répété *cent* **fois.**	You told me a hundred times.
J'ai *mille et une* **choses à faire.**	I have a thousand and one things to do.

3. In enumerations, if the nouns are understood to be all in the same category.

Ils ont invité *les parents, amis et connaissances* **des jeunes mariés.**	They have invited the parents, friends, and acquaintances of the newlyweds.

4. Before days, months, time of day, and some holidays.

Lundi prochain, **je vais chez**
  le médecin.
  Next Monday, I am going to
  the doctor.

Mai **est un joli mois.**
  May is a pretty month.

Midi **sonne.**
  It's striking noon.

Noël **au balcon,** *Pâques* **aux tisons.**
  Christmas on the balcony, Easter
  around a fire. (*old French saying*)

NOTE: When expressing a repeated action, the definite article is used with days of the week.

Le dimanche, **nous mangeons de la**
  pâtisserie au dessert.
  Every Sunday, we eat pastry
  for dessert.

NOTE: The article is used with *La Toussaint* (November 1st), *la Pentecôte* (Pentecost), and *le Mardi gras.*

5. In addresses.

Elle habite le boulevard
  Saint-Germain.
  She lives on Saint-Germain
  Boulevard.

The Partitive

The partitive, *du (m.), de la (f.), de l' (m. & f.),* and *des (plural),* meaning "some," is used before nouns that cannot be counted or that indicate an undetermined quantity.

Je mange *du pain, du beurre* **et** *de*
  la confiture **au petit déjeuner.**
  I eat bread, butter, and jam
  for breakfast.

Donne-moi *des fruits.*
  Give me some fruit.

Il a bu *de l'eau* **toute la**
  journée.
  He drank water all day.

The negative is expressed with *de* ("any").

Veux-tu *du pâté?*
  Do you want pâté?

Merci, je *ne* **veux** *pas*
  de pâté.
  No, thank you, I don't want
  any pâté.

16. Nouns

Gender

All nouns in French are either masculine or feminine. For nouns denoting things, the gender is purely coincidental. For people and animals, the gender is determined by the sex. The two nouns may then be entirely different or belong to the same family.

People

le fils son	la fille daughter
le garçon boy	la fille girl
l'homme (m.) man	la femme woman
le héros hero	l'héroïne (f.) heroine
le dieu god	la déesse goddess
l'oncle (m.) uncle	la tante aunt

Animals

le cheval horse	la jument mare
le coq rooster	la poule hen
le singe monkey	la guenon monkey
le taureau bull	la vache cow

1. Some nouns have the same form in both masculine and feminine.

l'artiste (m.)	l'artiste (f.)	artist
le camarade	la camarade	friend, comrade
le touriste	la touriste	tourist

2. In many cases, the feminine form of a noun is formed by adding an -e to the masculine form.

le cousin	la cousine	cousin
l'ami (m.)	l'amie (f.)	friend
l'étudiant (m.)	l'étudiante (f.)	student

3. Some masculine nouns ending in -n or -t double the consonant before adding an -e to form the feminine.

le lion	la lionne	lion, lioness
le paysan	la paysanne	peasant
le chat	la chatte	cat
le cadet	la cadette	the youngest

4. The feminine form of a noun ending in -*er* is formed with -*ère*.

le boulanger	**la boulangère**	baker
l'étranger (*m.*)	**l'étrangère** (*f.*)	stranger, foreigner
l'ouvrier (*m.*)	**l'ouvrière** (*f.*)	worker
le couturier	**la couturière**	fashion designer

5. The feminine form of a noun ending in -*eur* can be formed with -*euse*.

le coiffeur	**la coiffeuse**	hairdresser
le danseur	**la danseuse**	dancer
le menteur	**la menteuse**	liar

Some masculine nouns ending in -*teur* end in -*trice* in the feminine.

le directeur	**la directrice**	director
l'inspecteur	**l'inspectrice**	inspector
le manipulateur	**la manipulatrice**	manipulator

A few nouns in -*eur* do not have feminine forms, even when describing a female.

le chauffeur   driver
le professeur   teacher, professor
le docteur   doctor

NOTE: There is, however, now a trend to say *la prof*.

6. Some feminine nouns are formed by adding -*sse* to the masculine form.

le maître	master	**la maîtresse**	mistress
l'âne (*m.*)	donkey	**l'anesse** (*f.*)	donkey
le comte	count	**la comtesse**	countess
l'hôte (*m.*)	host	**l'hôtesse** (*f.*)	hostess
le prince	prince	**la princesse**	princess

7. A few nouns, whether referring to male or female, are always feminine.

une relation   an acquaintance
la personne   person
la victime   victim

8. A few nouns, whether referring to male or female, are always masculine.

l'auteur (*m.*)	author	**le peintre**	painter
le diplomate	diplomat	**le poète**	poet
l'écrivain (*m.*)	writer	**le soldat**	soldier
le juge	judge	**le témoin**	witness

9. A noun ending in -*f* changes to -*ve* in the feminine form.

le juif	**la juive**	Jew
le veuf	**la veuve**	widower, widow

10. Most nouns ending in -*x* change to -*se* in the feminine.

l'époux (*m.*)	**l'épouse** (*f.*)	spouse
l'orgueilleux (*m.*)	**l'orgueilleuse** (*f.*)	proud one

Plural of Nouns

The plural of nouns is usually formed by adding -*s* to the singular form. This is true of both masculine and feminine nouns.

la maison	house	**les maisons**	houses
le patron	boss	**les patrons**	bosses
la patronne	boss	**les patronnes**	bosses

1. Nouns ending in -*s*, -*x*, or -*z* do not change in the plural.

le pois	pea	**les pois**	peas
la croix	cross	**les croix**	crosses
le fils	son	**les fils**	sons
le nez	nose	**les nez**	noses

2. Nouns ending in -*al* change to -*aux* in the plural.

le canal	canal	**les canaux**	canals
le journal	newspaper	**les journaux**	newspapers
l'hôpital (*m.*)	hospital	**les hôpitaux**	hospitals

NOTE: *Le bal, le carnaval, le festival take an -s (les bals, les carnavals, les festivals).*

3. Nouns ending in -*au*, -*eau*, or -*eu* take an -*x* in the plural.

le noyau	pit (of a fruit)	**les noyaux**	pits
le manteau	coat	**les manteaux**	coats
le jeu	game	**les jeux**	games

4. Nouns ending in -*ou* take an -*s* in the plural, with the exception of these seven nouns:

le bijou	**les bijoux**	jewel(s)
le caillou	**les cailloux**	pebble(s)
le chou	**les choux**	cabbage(s)
le genou	**les genoux**	knee(s)
le hibou	**les hiboux**	owl(s)
le joujou	**les joujoux**	little toy(s)
le pou	**les poux**	louse (lice)

5. A few nouns have totally irregular plurals.

le ciel	sky	**les cieux**	heavens
l'œil	eye	**les yeux**	eyes

6. Nouns ending in -*ail* form the plural with -*s* except for a few.

le travail	work	**les travaux**	works
le vitrail	stained glass window	**les vitraux**	stained glass windows

7. Some nouns are usually used in the plural.

les ciseaux (*m.*)	scissors	les gens (*m.*)	people
les environs (*m.*)	surroundings	les lunettes (*f.*)	eyeglasses
les fiançailles (*f.*)	engagement	les mathématiques (*f.*)	mathematics
les frais (*m.*)	expenses	les mœurs (*f.*)	mores, customs
les funérailles (*f.*)	funeral	les vacances (*f.*)	vacation

NOTE: *Le ciseau* ("chisel"), *la lunette* (a kind of telescope), and *la vacance* ("vacancy") carry different meanings in the singular.

8. Some nouns are composed of two words. These nouns form their plurals like other nouns.

un pourboire	des pourboires	tips
un passeport	des passeports	passports
un portefeuille	des portefeuilles	wallets

Others form their plurals with the two words.

monsieur sir	messieurs sirs	
madame lady	mesdames ladies	
mademoiselle miss	mesdemoiselles misses (young ladies)	
un bonhomme chap	des bonshommes chaps	
un gentilhomme gentleman	des gentilshommes gentlemen	

9. The various rules (and their exceptions) for the plural formation of compound nouns are so complex, even for a French speaker, that only a few general statements will be made here.

Some compound nouns composed of adjectives and nouns pluralize both parts of the compound.

le beau-frère	les beaux-frères	brothers-in-law
le chou-fleur	les choux-fleurs	cauliflowers
le cerf-volant	les cerfs-volants	kites
le rouge-gorge	les rouges-gorges	robins
le coffre-fort	les coffres-forts	safes

NOTE: The adjective *grand* does not change in the feminine plural of compound nouns.

les grand-mères	grandmothers
les grand-tantes	great-aunts

Some compound nouns composed of verbs and nouns do not change in the plural.

le casse-cou	les casse-cou	daredevils
le gratte-ciel	les gratte-ciel	skyscrapers
le rendez-vous	les rendez-vous	appointments
le coupe-papier	les coupe-papier	letter openers
le pare-brise	les pare-brise	windshields

Some compounds composed of verbs and nouns pluralize the noun only.

le couvre-lit	les couvre-lits	bedspreads
le passe-montagne	les passe-montagnes	ski masks
le pique-nique	les pique-niques	picnics

The following compound nouns take an -*s* in the singular; they do not change in the plural.

le casse-noisettes   nutcracker
le cure-dents   toothpick
le chasse-mouches   flyswatter
le porte-avions   aircraft carrier
le porte-bagages   luggage rack
le porte-parapluies   umbrella stand
le presse-papiers   paperweight

Compound nouns that contain a preposition are often invariable.

le, les pied-à-terre   temporary lodging
le, les tête-à-tête   private conversations
le, les hors-d'œuvre   appetizers

But:

le chef-d'œuvre, les chefs-d'œuvre   masterpieces
l'arc-en-ciel, les arcs-en-ciel (*m.*)   rainbows

In a compound noun that contains an invariable word, that word always remains invariable.

l'après-midi (*m.*)	les après-midi	afternoons

An adjective that is part of a compound noun is pluralized.

le nouveau-venu	les nouveaux-venus	newcomers
le dernier-né	les derniers-nés	last born children

But:

le nouveau-né	les nouveau-nés the newly born

10. In general, words borrowed from other languages take an -*s* in the plural.

l'agenda (*m.*)	les agendas	le club	les clubs
l'album (*m.*)	les albums	le forum	les forums
l'alibi (*m.*)	les alibis	la jeep	les jeeps
l'auditorium (*m.*)	les auditoriums		

But the following can also be found:

un maximum	des maxima	un erratum	des errata

NOTE: For the sake of accuracy, it is best to consult a dictionary to check the current usage in the plural formation of a specific compound noun.

17. Adjectives and Adverbs

Adjectives

Agreement of Adjectives

An adjective (or a past participle used as an adjective) agrees in gender and number with the noun or the pronoun it modifies, whether as a direct modifier or as a predicate adjective. An adjective modifying nouns of different genders is in the masculine plural.

le cahier *vert*	the green notebook
la robe *verte*	the green dress
les cahiers *verts*	the green notebooks
les robes *vertes*	the green dresses
Le cahier est *vert.*	The notebook is green.
La robe est *verte.*	The dress is green.
Le cahier et la robe sont *verts.*	The notebook and the dress are green.

NOTE: Adjectives of color follow the noun. When two adjectives of color are used, one qualifying the other, they are both invariable.

les yeux *bleu clair*	light blue eyes
des robes *vert foncé*	dark green dresses

Gender of Adjectives

The feminine of an adjective is usually formed by adding -*e* to the masculine form.

Le panier est *rond.*	The basket is round.
La table est *ronde.*	The table is round.
Il est *grand.*	It is big.
Elle est *grande.*	It is big.

1. An adjective that ends in -*e* in the masculine singular does not change in the feminine.

le cahier *rouge,* la jupe *rouge*	the red notebook, the red skirt
le garçon *belge,* la femme *belge*	the Belgian boy, the Belgian woman

2. Adjectives that end in -*el,* -*eil,* or -*nul* in the masculine singular double the -*l* before adding -*e* to form the feminine. This is also true of *gentil.*

gentil	gentille	nice
nul	nulle	not one
cruel	cruelle	cruel
vermeil	vermeille	vermilion, bright red

3. Some adjectives have alternate masculine singular forms that are used before a word beginning with a vowel or a mute *h*.

masc. sing.	alt. masc. sing.	fem. sing.	masc. plur.	fem. plur.	
beau	bel	belle	beaux	belles	beautiful
fou	fol	folle	fous	folles	crazy
mou	mol	molle	mous	molles	soft
nouveau	nouvel	nouvelle	nouveaux	nouvelles	new
vieux	vieil	vieille	vieux	vieilles	old

4. Adjectives that end in *-en* and *-on* double the *n* before adding *-e* to form the feminine.

algérien, algérienne   Algerian
ancien, ancienne   ancient, former
bon, bonne   good
breton, bretonne   from Brittany
moyen, moyenne   average

5. Most adjectives ending in *-et* or *-l* double the *t* or *l* before adding *-e* to form the feminine.

muet, muette   silent, mute
net, nette   clean, spotless
quel, quelle   which, what
tel, telle   such

NOTE: *Complet* ("complete"), *incomplet* ("incomplete"), *concret* ("concrete"), *discret* ("discreet"), *indiscret* ("indiscreet"), *inquiet* ("worried"), and *secret* ("secret") take the ending *-ète: complet, complète.*

6. Most adjectives that end in *-s* in the masculine singular take an *-e* in the feminine form.

gris, grise   gray

But the following adjectives double the *s* before adding *-e*.

bas, basse   low   **gras, grasse**   fat
épais, épaisse   thick   **gros, grosse**   big, stout

NOTE: *Frais* becomes *fraîche.*

7. An adjective ending in *-x* in the masculine singular changes to *-se*.

heureux, heureuse   happy
jaloux, jalouse   jealous

NOTE: *Faux* ("false") and *roux* ("reddish-brown") become *fausse* and *rousse.*

8. A few adjectives whose masculine forms end in *-f* change to *-ve* in the feminine.

actif, active   active   **neuf, neuve**   new
bref, brève   brief   **vif, vive**   alive, lively
captif, captive   captive

9. Some adjectives whose masculine forms end in -c change the -c to -que in the feminine.

public, publique public

NOTE: *Blanc* ("white") and *franc* ("frank") become *blanche* and *franche; sec* ("dry") becomes *sèche.*

10. Adjectives ending in -g in the masculine singular change to -gue.

long, longue long
oblong, oblongue oblong

11. Adjectives ending in -gu add -ë.

aigu, aiguë sharp
ambigu, ambiguë ambiguous

12. Most adjectives ending in -eur have the feminine forms -euse or -trice.

menteur, menteuse lying
trompeur, trompeuse deceptive, misleading
voleur, voleuse thieving

producteur, productrice productiv
protecteur, protectrice protective

NOTE: *Antérieur, postérieur, ultérieur, extérieur, intérieur, majeur, mineur, supérieur, inférieur,* and *meilleur* form the feminine with -e.

13. A small number of adjectives are irregular.

favori, favorite favorite
malin, maligne shrewd, cunning
rigolo, rigolote funny

Number

The plural of most adjectives is formed by adding -s to the singular (masculine or feminine) form. All feminine adjectives have regular plurals. Only masculine adjectives are irregular.

1. Masculine adjectives ending in -s or -x do not change in the plural.

un manteau gris **des manteaux gris** gray coats
un vent doux **des vents doux** soft winds

2. A masculine adjective ending in -eau takes -x in the plural.

un beau chapeau **de beaux chapeaux** beautiful hats
un nouveau parapluie **de nouveaux parapluies** new umbrellas

NOTE: A plural noun preceded by a plural adjective takes *de* instead of *des.*

3. Adjectives ending in -al generally change to -aux.

un soldat loyal **des soldats loyaux** loyal soldiers

NOTE: But *naval* ("naval"), *fatal* ("fatal"), *natal* ("native"), and *final* ("final") take -s.

4. *Tout* ("all") has the plural *tous.*

Position of Adjectives

1. In general, a descriptive adjective follows the noun it modifies.

un lion féroce   a ferocious lion   **une pièce immense**   a huge room
un homme sérieux   a serious man

2. Some descriptive adjectives precede the noun.

une belle maison	a beautiful house	**un vieux chat**	an old cat
une bonne journée	a good day	**un joli arbre**	a pretty tree
un vilain tableau	an ugly painting	**une nouvelle maison**	a new house

3. Certain descriptive adjectives are placed before or after the noun, depending on their meaning.

une maison ancienne	an old house	**un grand homme**	a great man
une ancienne amie	a former friend	**un homme grand**	a tall man
une chambre propre	a clean room	**un homme brave**	a brave man
ma propre chambre	my own room	**un brave homme**	a fine
la semaine dernière	last week (the week		(good) man
	before)	**une histoire vraie**	a true story
la dernière semaine	the last week (of a	**une vraie bête**	a real beast
	series)	**un vieillard pauvre**	a poor
une voiture chère	an expensive car		(needy) man
un cher cousin	a dear cousin	**un pauvre vieillard**	a poor (to
une personne seule	a person alone		be pitied) man
une seule personne	only one person		

4. Indefinite adjectives usually come before the noun.

plusieurs	several	**autre**	other
chaque	every, each	**même**	same
quelque	some, a few	**tel, telle**	such
tout(e)	all	**certain**	certain

quelques object rares	a few rare objects
plusieurs choses	several things
toutes les mères	all the mothers

A few indefinite adjectives change meaning depending on their position.

l'idée même	the very idea	**une certaine réussite**	a certain amount of success
la même idée	the same idea	**une réussite certaine**	an unqualified success

Comparison of Adjectives

1. To form a comparative of inequality, place *plus* ("more") or *moins* ("less") before the adjective and *que* after the adjective. A comparative of equality is formed by placing *aussi* ("as") before the adjective and *que* after the adjective.

Inequality:

Marc est *plus grand que* **Catherine.**	Marc is taller than Catherine.
Catherine est *moins grande que* **Marc.**	Catherine is less tall than Marc.

Equality:

Marc est *aussi intelligent que* **Catherine.**	Marc is as intelligent as Catherine.
Catherine n'est pas *aussi sportive que* **Marc.**	Catherine is not as sportive as Marc.

2. To form the superlative, place the definite article before the comparative and *de* after the adjective.

C'est *le plus grand de* **tous.**	He is the tallest of them all.
Marc est *le plus grand* **élève** *de* **sa classe.**	Marc is the tallest student in his class.

Irregular Comparison

	Comparatives			Superlatives	
bon	**meilleur**	better	**le (la) meilleur(e)**	the best
mauvais	**pire**	worse	**le (la) pire**	the worst
petit	**moindre**	less (in importance)	**le (la) moindre**	the least

NOTE: In some cases, *plus mauvais* and *le plus mauvais* are used instead of *pire* and *le pire*. *Plus petit* and *le plus petit* are used to compare size.

Adverbs

Adverbs are invariable words that modify verbs.

Adverbs of Manner

1. Most adverbs of manner are formed by adding the suffix -*ment* to the feminine singular form of the adjective.

grave	**grave**	**gravement**	seriously
long	**longue**	**longuement**	for a long time, at length
complet	**complète**	**complètement**	completely
vif	**vive**	**vivement**	vivaciously

2. A few adjectives change the mute -*e* to -*é* before the suffix.

énorme	**énormément**	enormously
profonde	**profondément**	deeply

3. Usually, when the masculine form of the adjective ends with a vowel, -*ment* is added to the masculine form.

joli	**jolie**	**joliment**	prettily
vrai	**vraie**	**vraiment**	really

NOTE: *Gai (gaie),* however, becomes *gaiement* ("gaily").

4. Masculine singular adjectives ending in -*ant* and -*ent* form adverbs ending in -*amment* and -*emment* (which replace the -*nt* ending of the adjective).

suffisant	**suffisamment**	sufficiently
prudent	**prudemment**	prudently

NOTE: One common exception to this rule is *lent*.

lent	**lente**	**lentement**	slowly

5. Some common adverbs of manner not ending in -*ment* include:

ainsi	like this, thus	**plutôt**	rather
bien	well	**tard**	late
debout	up, standing	**tôt**	early
comme	how	**vite**	quickly
exprès	on purpose	**volontiers**	gladly
mal	badly	**ensemble**	together

Position of Adverbs of Manner

1. Adverbs modifying verbs in a simple tense are usually placed after the verb.

Je vous l'envoie directement.	I am sending it to you directly.

2. In perfect tenses, the position of adverbs varies: As a guideline, place adverbs of more than one syllable after the verb, and those of one syllable between the auxiliary and the past participle.

Je vous l'ai envoyé directement.	I sent it to you directly.

3. Short adverbs come before an infinitive.

Apprenez à bien conduire!	Learn to drive well!

4. Adverbs of manner are placed before the adjective or adverb they modify.

Elle est bien habillée.	She is well dressed.
Il parlait plutôt mal.	He spoke rather badly.

Comparison of Adverbs

Regular comparison of adverbs is like that of adjectives, with *plus, aussi,* and *moins* placed before the adverb and *que* after.

Inequality:

Je mange *moins mal* **ici** **qu'au restaurant.**	I eat less badly here than in a restaurant.
Nous voyageons *plus régulièrement* **que`l'année dernière.**	We are traveling more regularly than last year.

Equality:

Elle parle *aussi fort que* **son père.**	She speaks as loudly as her father.

Superlative:
Le plus souvent, **il dort après**   Most often, he sleeps after
   le repas.   meals.

Irregular Comparisons

Adverb	Comparative	Superlative
bien well	**mieux** better	**le mieux** the best
mal badly	**pis, plus mal** worse	**le pis, le plus mal** the worst
beaucoup much	**plus** more	**le plus** the most
peu little	**moins** less	**le moins** the least

NOTE: When a clause introduced by *que* follows an affirmative comparison of inequality, *ne* is used before the verb in the dependent clause.

Marie est *plus sportive que* **je**   Marie is more sportive than I
   ne **le croyais.**   thought.

Adverbs of Quantity

1. Adverbs of quantity are used with a verb, before a comparative, before a noun with *de,* and before the adverbs *plus, moins,* and *trop.*

assez enough

autant as much

beaucoup much, a lot

combien how much

ne...guère hardly

peu little

presque almost

davantage more

plus more

moins less

très very

trop too much

ne...pas du tout not at all

la plupart most

Il est *beaucoup* **plus**   He is much more talkative
   bavard que moi.   than I.
Je n'ai pas *assez* **d'argent.**   I don't have enough money.

2. *Bien des* is used in the sense of *beaucoup de.* It is followed by a noun.

Bien des **voyages se**   Many trips end badly.
   terminent mal.

3. *Aussi* is used before an adjective or an adverb.

Vous avez couru *aussi* **vite**   You ran as fast as I did.
   que moi.

NOTE: If the sentence is negative, *si* is used instead of *aussi.*

(adjective)
Elle n'est pas *si* **timide**   She is not as timid as
   que vous croyez.   you think.

(adverb)
Il ne travaille pas *si* **vite**   He doesn't work as fast as
   qu'il en a l'air.   he seems to.

18. Possession

Possession with *De*

A phrase with the preposition *de* ("of") followed by a person's name or a noun is used to indicate possession.

la voiture de Philippe	Philippe's car
la queue du chat	the cat's tail
la fleur du pommier	the apple tree's bloom

Possessive Adjectives

Possessive adjectives are placed before the noun and agree in number and gender with the thing possessed, not the possessor.

Masculine Singular	Feminine Singular	Masculine and Feminine Plural
mon, ton, son	ma, ta, sa	mes, tes, ses
my, your, his (her)	my, your, his (her)	my, your, his (her)
	notre, votre, leur	nos, vos, leurs
	our, your, their	our, your, their

mon crayon	my pencil	ses parents	his (her) parents
ton stylo	your pen	notre maison	our house
son frère	his (her) brother	votre appartement	your apartment
ma table	my table	leur mère	their mother
ta chaise	your chair	nos voitures	our cars
sa sœur	his (her) sister	vos télévisions	your televisions
mes cahiers	my notebooks	leurs parents	their parents
tes livres	your books		

NOTE: Before a noun beginning with a vowel or a mute *h*, the masculine forms *mon, ton,* and *son* are used instead of *ma, ta,* and *sa*.

mon aventure (*f.*)	my adventure
ton horloge (*f.*)	your clock
son équipe (*f.*)	his (her) team

The definite article is used instead of the possessive adjective when speaking of parts of the body. Note that the past participles in the following example sentences are invariable.

Il lui a tendu *les* bras.	He opened his arms to her.
Je vais me laver *les* mains.	I am going to wash my hands.
Elle s'est cassé *la* jambe.	She broke her leg.

Possessive Pronouns

The possessive pronouns are always preceded by a definite article and agree in gender and number with the thing possessed.

le mien, la mienne	mine	**les miens, les miennes**	mine
le tien, la tienne	yours	**les tiens, les tiennes**	yours
le sien, la sienne	his (hers)	**les siens, les siennes**	his (hers)
le nôtre, la nôtre	ours	**les nôtres**	ours
le vôtre, la vôtre	yours	**les vôtres**	yours
le leur, la leur	theirs	**les leurs**	theirs

Ma cravate est moche. Donne-moi *la tienne!*	My necktie is ugly. Give me yours!
Voilà *la mienne.*	Here is mine.
Mes parents vont bien. Et *les vôtres?*	My parents are well. And yours?

1. The definite articles *le* and *les* preceding possessive adjectives contract with *à* and *de.*

Ne parlons pas de mon travail. **Parlons** *du vôtre.*	Let's not talk about my work. Let's talk about yours.
A votre santé! A *la* **bonne** *vôtre!*	To your health! To yours!
J'ai écrit à mes parents. Mon cousin n'a pas écrit *aux siens.*	I have written my parents. My cousin has not written his.

2. To express possession with the verb *être*, one can also use the emphatic pronouns *moi, toi, lui, elle, nous, vous, eux,* and *elles.*

Ce stylo est *à toi?* **Non, il est** *à eux.*	This pen belongs to you? No, it's theirs.

3. Some idiomatic expressions with possessive adjectives and pronouns:

Il l'a fait *de son propre chef.*	He did it on his own initiative.
Dites-lui bien des choses *de ma part.*	Give him my best.
Elle était *des nôtres* **pour Noël.**	She was with us at Christmas time.

19. Demonstrative Adjectives and Pronouns

Demonstrative Adjectives

Singular		Plural
ce, cet (*m.*) } this, that		ces these, those
cette (*f.*) }		

The demonstrative adjective precedes and agrees in number and gender with the noun it modifies. The masculine form *cet* is used before a noun beginning with a vowel or a mute *h*.

ce matin	this (that) morning
cet été	this (that) summer
cette plage	this (that) beach
ces maillots de bain	these (those) swimming suits

1. When it is necessary to make a distinction between "this" and "that," or "these" and "those," -*ci* and -*là* may be added to the noun, -*ci* referring to things close to the speaker, *là* to things further away.

Ce plat-*ci* est meilleur que ce plat-*là*.	This dish is better than that dish.

2. Demonstrative adjectives must be repeated before each noun.

ce livre et cette lampe	this book and this lamp
ces garçons et ces filles	these boys and girls

However, when a noun is preceded by several descriptive adjectives applying to the noun, the demonstrative adjective is not repeated.

ce bel et bon seigneur	this beautiful and good lord

Demonstrative Pronouns

Singular		Plural	
celui (*m.*) } this, this one,		ceux (*m.*) } these, those	
celle (*f.*) } that, that one		celles (*f.*) }	

As-tu pris ton écharpe? Non, j'ai pris *celle* de Claudette.	Did you take your scarf? No, I took Claudette's.
Quel autobus vas-tu prendre? *Celui* qui passe boulevard Saint-Michel.	What bus are you going to take? The one that goes on Saint-Michel Boulevard.

1. A demonstrative pronoun always refers to someone or something mentioned previously. It is often followed by *-ci* or *-là* to convey the meaning of "this one" or "that one."

Quelle glace préfères-tu?	Which ice cream do you prefer?
Celle-ci **ou** *celle-là*?	This one or that one?

2. The demonstrative pronouns may be followed by the relative pronouns *qui, que,* or *dont.*

C'est *celui-là qui* **te plaît?**	Is it that one you like?
Celle que **je t'ai donnée est plus jolie.**	The one I gave you is prettier.
Ce sont *ceux dont* **je t'ai parlé.**	They are the ones I spoke to you about.

3. A demonstrative pronoun may be followed by *de* to indicate possession.

Voilà mon parapluie et voilà *celui de* **ma sœur.**	Here is my umbrella and here is the one that belongs to my sister (my sister's).

4. *Ceci* and *cela* are invariable pronouns that refer to facts, ideas, or things not named specifically.

Tout *ceci* **me chagrine.**	All this pains me.
Tout *cela* **m'est égal.**	I don't care about all that.

5. *Ce* may be used as an invariable demonstrative pronoun and translated as "it," "he," "she," "this," "that," "they," "these," "those."

Ce is used as subject of the verb *être* when the verb is followed by a modified noun, a proper noun, a pronoun, or a superlative.

Modified noun:

C'est un grand homme.	He is a great man.
Ce fut une fête mémorable.	It was a memorable party.

NOTE: The personal pronouns *il, ils, elle,* and *elles* are used when *être* is followed by an adjective or a noun by itself.

Il est grand.	He is tall.
Elle est médecin.	She is a physician.

Proper noun:

C'est Claude qui a écrit.	It was Claude who wrote.
Qui est-ce? C'est Simone.	Who is it? It's Simone.

Demonstrative and possessive pronoun:

C'est celui-là que j'aime.	It's that one I like.
C'est le vôtre?	Is it yours?

Superlative and *seul:*

C'est le plus grand homme que j'aie rencontré.	That's the tallest man I have ever met.
Est-ce le seul que vous ayez?	Is it the only one you have?

NOTE: *Ce* before *être* often repeats a subject already expressed.

Mon meilleur ami, c'est vous.	My best friend is you.
Les plats que je préfère, ce sont	The dishes I prefer are those
les plats préparés en sauce.	prepared with a sauce.
Partir, c'est mourir un peu.	To leave is to die a little.

Ce is used with *être* when the verb is followed by an adjective modified by an infinitive. The infinitive, then, is preceded by the preposition *à*.

Ce n'est pas facile à faire.	It's not easy to do.
C'était difficile à deviner.	It was difficult to guess.

Ce can be used when the verb *être* is preceded by the verbs *devoir, pouvoir,* or *aller*.

Ce doit être une plaisanterie.	It must be a joke.
Ce peut être une erreur.	It could be a mistake.

NOTE: The impersonal pronoun *il* is used when *être* is followed by an adjective, itself modified by an infinitive, to represent a concept or an idea. In this case, the infinitive is preceded by *de*. If the concept applies to another person, *que* is used, followed by the subjunctive.

Il est préférable de partir tout	It is preferable to leave
de suite.	right away.
Il est préférable que tu partes	It is preferable that you leave
tout de suite.	right away.

6. *Ça,* a reduced form of *cela,* is invariable and is used commonly in various expressions.

Ça y est.	That's it.
À part ça	Aside from that
Ça suffit.	That's enough.
Ça a l'air d'une soucoupe volante!	It looks like a flying saucer.
Ça va? Ça va mal.	How are things? Things are not going well.
Ne faites pas ça!	Don't do that!
C'est comme ça.	That's the way it is.
Comme ci comme ça.	So-so.
C'est pour ça.	That's why.
Comment ça se fait?	How come?
Ça ne fait rien!	It doesn't matter!

20. Personal Pronouns

Subject Pronouns

A subject pronoun is the subject of a verb. The speaker is called the first person; the one spoken to is the second person; and the one spoken of is the third person.

	Singular	Plural
1st person	**je (j')** I	**nous** we
2nd person	**tu** you	**vous** you
3rd person	**il, elle, on** he, she, one (we, etc.)	**ils, elles** they

1. *On* is a convenient indefinite pronoun used only as a subject. Commonly used in everyday conversation, it can have the meaning of "we," "someone," "one," "people," "everyone." In writing, it can also mean "I," "he," "she," "you," "they." When *on* is used with *être* and an adjective, the adjective takes the number and gender of the person or persons represented by *on*.

On va au cinéma?	Shall we go to the movies?
On était petites à cette époque-là.	We (girls) were little at the time.

2. In French there are two pronouns used to express "you": *tu* and *vous*. The familiar *tu* is used to address relatives, friends, classmates, children, and animals. *Vous* is used when speaking to an adult, a stranger, or more than one person.

Marc, as-tu fini de taquiner ton frère?	Marc, will you stop teasing your brother?
Bonjour, Madame Ogier. Comment allez-vous?	Good morning, Mrs. Ogier How are you?
Bonjour, mes enfants. Comment allez-vous?	Good morning, children. How are you?

3. *Il* and *elle* stand for persons ("he," "she") as well as for animals and inanimate objects ("it"). The gender of the pronoun is the same as the gender of the noun it replaces.

Jean **se promène avec son chien.** *Il* **en est très fier.**	Jean is taking a walk with his dog. He is very proud of him.
J'aime *la vitesse,* **mais** *elle* **tue.**	I like speed, but it kills.
Ma chatte **est gourmande.** *Elle* **mange toute la journée.**	My cat is a glutton. She eats all day long.

Emphatic Pronouns

Corresponding to the subject pronouns, the emphatic pronouns are:

moi	nous
toi	vous
lui	eux
elle	elles
soi	

1. The emphatic pronouns are used to emphasize the subject or the object pronoun.

J'habite à Paris. Et *toi?*	I live in Paris. And you?
Où est-ce que tu l'as connu, *lui?*	Where did you meet *him?*

2. An emphatic pronoun is used after a preposition.

Voulez-vous vous promener *avec moi?*	Do you want to go for a walk with me?
Mettez-vous *derrière lui.*	Go behind him.

3. The emphatic pronouns are used after verbs that take the prepositions *à* and *de* and after verbs of motion.

Je penserai *à toi.*	I'll think of you.
Laissez venir *à moi* **les petits enfants.**	Let the little children come to me.
Il se méfie *de toi.*	He is suspicious of you.

4. An emphatic pronoun may be part of a sentence without a verb.

Qui a mangé le gâteau? *Pas moi.*	Who ate the cake? Not I.

5. An emphatic pronoun can be used with *ce* and *être*.

Qui est le plus bête? *C'est lui.*	Who is the stupidest? It's him.
Ce sont eux **qui le disent.**	It's they who say so.

6. In comparisons, or with *ni. . .ni* or *ne. . .que,* emphatic pronouns are used.

Michel est plus intelligent que *lui.*	Michel is smarter than he.
Je n'aime que *toi.*	I love only you.
Je n'inviterai *ni lui ni elle.*	I'll invite neither him nor her.

7. The emphatic pronouns are used after commands. When *en* is used, *moi* and *toi* become *m'* and *t'*.

Écoute-moi!	Listen to me!
Parlez-m'en!	Talk to me about it!

8. *Soi* is used after a preposition when the subject of the verb is *on, chacun,* or *personne*.

Chacun pour soi.	To each his own.
On n'a jamais confiance qu'en soi-même.	One only trusts oneself.

9. *Même* after an emphatic pronoun is used to emphasize even more that it is the person talked about who did the action, and conveys the idea of "self" in English.

Je préfère le faire *moi-même.*	I prefer to do it myself.
C'est *eux-mêmes* **qui me l'ont dit.**	They told me themselves.

Reflexive Pronouns

Reflexive pronouns are those used with pronominal verbs. (See Chapter 4.) They, too, correspond to the subject pronouns.

me	nous
te	vous
se	se

Se is also used with the infinitive: *s'habiller* ("to get dressed"), *se lever* ("to get up").

Nous nous amusons **à la ville.**	We enjoy ourselves in town.
Vous vous ennuyez **à la campagne.**	You are getting bored in the country.

Direct Object Pronouns

The direct object pronoun receives the action of the verb. It is placed before the verb.

me	me	nous	us
te	you	vous	you
le	him, it	les	them
la	her, it		

Si tu n'es pas gentil, je ne *t'*aimerai plus.	If you are not nice, I won't love you any more.
Ma vieille robe? Je *l'*ai donnée aux pauvres.	My old dress? I gave it to the poor.
Le jeune chien *la* **léchait gentiment.**	The young dog licked her gently.

Indirect Object Pronouns

The indirect object pronoun denotes the person to, for, or from whom something is given, told, sent, etc. It is placed before the verb.

me	to me	nous	to us
te	to you	vous	to you
lui	to him, to her	leur	to them

Maman va *leur* **téléphoner.**	Mom is going to phone them.
Je *lui* **ai donné leur numéro de téléphone.**	I gave her their telephone number.
Est-ce que je *te* **l'ai donné aussi?**	Did I give it to you also?

Table of Personal Pronouns

Subject	Direct Object	Indirect Object	Reflexive	Emphatic
je (j')	me (m')	me (m')	me (m')	moi
tu	te (t')	te (t')	te (t')	toi
il	le (l')	lui	se (s')	lui
elle	la (l')	lui	se (s')	elle
on			se (s')	soi
nous	nous	nous	nous	nous
vous	vous	vous	vous	vous
ils	les	leur	se (s')	eux
elles	les	leur	se (s')	elles

Y and En

As a pronoun, *y* refers to places, things, or ideas that have already been mentioned. *Y* often replaces *à* (or another preposition) + a place, thing, or idea.

Vas-tu à la banque? Oui, j'*y* **vais.**	Are you going to the bank? Yes, I'm going there.
Est-il derrière le garage? Non, il n'*y* **est pas.**	Is he behind the garage? No, he is not there.
Pensez-vous aller au théâtre? Oui, j'*y* **pense.**	Are you thinking of going to the theater? Yes, I'm thinking about it.

En refers to things, places, and ideas. It often replaces *de* + a noun.

Des lions? Il *en* **a tué beaucoup.**	Lions? He killed a lot of them.
Tu as des disques de jazz? Oui, j'*en* **ai une douzaine.**	Do you have jazz records? Yes, I have a dozen of them.
Vous sortez de l'école à 3 h? Oui, nous *en* **sortons à 3 h.**	Do you leave school at three o'clock? Yes, we leave (there) at three o'clock.

Double Object Pronouns

More than one object pronoun may be used in a sentence. In that case, the pronouns appear in a certain order before the verb.

me					
te	le (l')	lui			
se	la (l')	leur	y	en	*verb*
nous	les				
vous					

Je *le lui* **ai dit hier.**	I said it to him yesterday.
Nous *lui en* **avons parlé hier.**	We spoke to him about it yesterday.
Tu *les y* **as vues?**	Did you see them there?
Ne *m'en* **parle pas!**	Don't tell me about that!

Order After the Verb

Object pronouns are placed after the verb in an affirmative imperative sentence.

		moi		
		toi		
	le	lui		
verb	la	nous	y	en
	les	vous		
		leur		

Offre-*lui* **des bonbons!**	Give him candy! Give him a lot!
Offre-*lui-en* **beaucoup!**	
Vends-*les-leur!* **Ils ne nous font**	Sell them to them! They never
jamais de cadeaux!	give us any presents!
Apporte-*moi* **la bouteille, mais**	Bring me the bottle, but don't
ne la casse pas!	break it!

21. Relative Pronouns

A relative pronoun occurs in a dependent clause and describes or refers to a noun or a group of words in the main clause.

	Simple Forms		Compound Forms			
			Singular		Plural	
			Masc.	Femi.	Masc.	Femi.
who, that, which	qui	which	lequel	laquelle	lesquels	lesquelles
whom, that, which	que	of which	duquel	de laquelle	desquels	desquelles
of whom, of which	dont	to which	auquel	à laquelle	auxquels	auxquelles

Simple Forms

1. *Qui* is used as the subject of the verb, *que* as the object. *Dont* replaces *de* + a form of *lequel*.

C'est une de mes cousines *qui* m'a invitée à la campagne.	It's one of my cousins who invited me to the country.
C'est le bateau *que* je voulais acheter.	It's the boat I wanted to buy.
As-tu entendu le concert *qu'*on a donné hier à la télé?	Did you hear the concert that was on TV yesterday?
Voilà le journal *dont* je vous ai parlé.	Here is the newspaper I talked to you about.

2. *Où* can be used as a relative pronoun to refer to an antecedent of time or place.

C'est là *où* j'aimerais aller.	That's where I would like to go.
C'est l'année *où* j'ai gagné un prix.	It was the year I won a prize.

Compound Forms

1. The forms of *lequel* can be the object of a preposition and usually refer to things, although they may also be used for people.

C'est la raison *pour laquelle* on l'a renvoyé.	That's the reason for which he was fired.

2. *De* and *lequel* contract to become *duquel*. *Duquel* is often replaced by *dont*.

Le grand livre sur la table? *Duquel* parlez-vous?	The big book on the table? Which one are you talking about?

3. *Auquel* is a contraction of *à* + *lequel*. It is often replaced by *à qui* when referring to people.

C'est une chose *à laquelle* **tu aurais dû penser.**	That's something you should have thought about.
Le garçon *auquel (à qui)* **tu parlais est portugais.**	The boy you were talking to is Portuguese.

4. *Ce qui, ce que,* and *ce dont* are used when the antecedent is not precise, or is understood. *Ce qui* is the subject of the verb. *Ce que* is the object. *Ce dont* is used when the verb takes *de.*

Ce qui **t'appartient m'appartient.**	What belongs to you belongs to me.
Montre-moi *ce que* **tu as trouvé.**	Show me what you found.
Je ne suis pas d'accord avec *ce dont* **tu parles.**	I don't agree with what you are talking about.

NOTE: With *tout,* these forms express the idea of "all that" or "everything."

Tout ce qui **brille n'est pas d'or.**	All that glitters is not gold.
Je te donnerai *tout ce que* **tu voudras.**	I'll give you everything you want.

22. Interrogatives and Exclamations

Interrogatives

Interrogatives are classified as pronouns, adjectives, and adverbs.

Pronouns

	Persons		Things		Persons and Things	
Subject of the Question						
	qui	who			lequel	
	qui est-ce qui	who	qu'est-ce qui	what	laquelle	which, which one
					lesquels	
					lesquelles	
Direct Object						
	qui	whom	que	what	lequel	
	qui est-ce que	whom	qu'est-ce que	what	laquelle	which, which one
					lesquels	
					lesquelles	
Object of a Preposition						
	qui	whom	quoi	what	lequel	
					laquelle	which, which one
					lesquels	
					lesquelles	

Qui m'attend?	Who is waiting for me?
Qui est-ce qui m'attend?	Who is waiting for me?
Qui attendez-vous?	Whom are you waiting for?
Qui est-ce que vous attendez?	Whom are you waiting for?
A qui avez-vous écrit?	To whom did you write?
Qu'est-ce qui vous ennuie?	What is bothering you?
Que vais-je faire?	What am I going to do?
Qu'est-ce qu'elle dit?	What is she saying?
A quoi pensez-vous?	What are you thinking about?
Lequel d'entre vous a fait ça?	Which one of you did that?
Laquelle allons-nous acheter?	Which one are we going to buy?
Desquels vous servirez-vous?	Which ones will you use?

1. When *qui, que,* and *quoi* are used as direct objects or are preceded by a preposition, there is inversion of the subject and verb.

Qui êtes-vous?	Who are you?
Que dis-je?	What am I saying?
Que puis-je faire pour vous?	What can I do for you?
Pour qui me prenez-vous?	Who do you think I am?

2. The forms *qui est-ce qui, qu'est-ce qui, qui est-ce que,* and *qu'est-ce que* do not call for inversion.

Qu'est-ce qui s'est passé?	What happened?
Qui est-ce qui te l'a dit?	Who told you so?

3. The forms of *lequel* always refer to someone or something that has to be chosen among others.

Voilà deux portes. Par laquelle entrerons-nous?	Here are two doors. Which one shall we go through?
Parmi tous ces vélos, lequel vas-tu acheter?	Among all these bikes, which one are you going to buy?
De tous vos amis étrangers, lesquels préférez-vous?	Of all your foreign friends, which ones do you prefer?

4. All three forms of *lequel* contract with *à* or *de.*

Un dentiste? Auquel vous adresserez-vous?	A dentist? Which one will you go to?
Vos cousines? Desquelles parlez-vous?	Your cousins? Which ones are you speaking of?

5. The pronoun *quoi* can sometimes be the subject of the question.

Quoi de plus facile?	**What is easier?**
Quoi d'autre?	**What else?**

6. *À qui* used with *être* shows ownership; *de qui* used with *être* expresses personal relationship or authorship.

A qui est ce tablier?	Whose apron is it?
De qui est ce livre?	Who is the author of this book?
De quoi êtes-vous fait?	What are you made of?

Adjectives

1. *Quel, quelle, quels, quelles* ("which," "what") are the forms of the interrogative adjectives. They agree in number and gender with the nouns they modify.

Quelles nouvelles m'apportez-vous?	What news did you bring me?
A quel hôtel descendrez-vous?	What hotel will you go to?

2. Used with the verb *être,* the interrogative adjective may be separated from the noun it modifies.

Quel est ce bruit?	What is that noise?

Adverbs

quand when	**d'où** from where
pendant combien de temps how long	**par où** from where
depuis combien de temps since when (length)	**pourquoi** why
depuis quand since when (date)	**comment** how
où where	**combien** how much, how many

Quand arrives-tu?	When are you coming?
Où irez-vous?	Where will you go?
Pourquoi partent-ils?	Why are they leaving?
Combien as-tu payé?	How much did you pay?

Exclamations

The forms of *quel* are used as exclamatory adjectives.

Quelle chance!	What luck!
Quel beau bateau!	What a beautiful boat!
Quels idiots!	What idiots!

Comme, combien, and *que* are also used in exclamations.

Comme il est beau!	How beautiful it is!
Vous ne pouvez pas savoir combien je l'aime!	You can't imagine how much I love her!
Que je suis content!	How glad I am!

23. Some Practical Rules

Question Formation

There are several ways to form questions in French. The sentence construction may be changed or the speaker's intonation may change.

1. One may form a question using the construction of a declarative sentence, but with rising intonation. This is very common in conversation.

Vous allez à l'église tous les dimanches? — You go to church every Sunday?

2. You may add *n'est-ce-pas?* to a declarative sentence, with rising intonation. This form is asking for confirmation.

Vous allez à l'église tous les dimanches, *n'est-ce-pas?* — You go to church every Sunday, don't you?

NOTE: *N'est-ce-pas?* is invariable.

3. *Est-ce que* may precede a declarative sentence (rising intonation). This formula is often used in conversation.

Est-ce que **vous allez à l'église tous les dimanches?** — Do you go to church every Sunday?

4. One may form an interrogative sentence using inversion. This formula is used more in writing than in conversation.

Allez-vous **à l'église tous les dimanches?** — Do you go to church every Sunday?

NOTE: The formula with *est-ce que* can be modified into *est-ce. . .qui, c'est . . .qui,* or *est-ce que c'est. . .qui.*

Est-ce vous *qui* m'avez écrit? — Is it you who wrote me?
C'est lui *qui* a parlé le premier? — Is it he who spoke first?
Est-ce que c'est elle *qui* lui a répondu? — Is it she who answered him?

Indirect Statements

An indirect statement may be reported in the present or the past. When reported in the present, the tense of the original (direct) statement does not change. When reported in the past, the tenses change according to the tense used in the original (direct) statement.

Present: Pierre dit: "Je suis content."   Pierre dit qu'il est content.
Pierre dit: "Je finirai mon   Pierre dit qu'il finira son
   travail ce soir."   travail ce soir.
Pierre dit: "J'ai fini mon   Pierre dit qu'il a fini son
   travail."   travail.

Past: Pierre a dit: "Je suis content."   Pierre a dit qu'il était content.
Pierre a dit: "Je finirai   Pierre a dit qu'il finirait
   mon travail ce soir."   son travail ce soir.
Pierre a dit: "J'ai fini   Pierre a dit qu'il avait
   mon travail."   fini son travail.

An interrogation is called indirect when the speaker is reporting a question asked by him or her or by a third party.

Direct: **Quand allez-vous arriver?**
Indirect: **Pierre m'a demandé quand on allait arriver.**

Direct: **Où est-ce que vous serez à huit heures?**
Indirect: **Pierre m'a demandé où nous serons à huit heures.**

Direct: **Prendrez-vous un taxi?**
Indirect: **Pierre m'a demandé si on prendrait un taxi.**

NOTE: There is no inversion in indirect questions.

24. Negatives

Non

Non is the adverb of negation most commonly used in French.

Apportez-vous de bonnes nouvelles?	Are you bringing good news?
Non.	No.
Veux-tu encore du dessert?	Do you want more dessert?
Non, **j'en ai déjà repris.**	No, I have already had seconds.

NOTE: After a negative statement or question, *si* is used instead of *oui*.

Tu n'as pas de voiture?	You don't have a car?
Mais *si.* **J'ai celle de Marc.**	Of course I do. I have Marc's.

Other Common Negatives

ne...pas	not	**ne...ni...ni**	neither...nor
ne...pas du tout	not at all	**ne...ni ne**	neither...nor
ne...point	not, not at all	**ne...que**	only
ne...plus	not any more, no more, no longer	**ne...aucun(e)**	no, none, no one
		ne...nul(le)	no, none, no one
ne...guère	hardly, scarcely	**ne...aucunement**	not at all, not in any way
ne...personne	no one, nobody		
ne...rien	nothing	**ne...nullement**	not at all, by no means

Qu'est-ce qu'il y a là-dedans?	What's in there? Nothing.
Il *n'*y a *rien.*	
Vous avez des frères et des sœurs?	Do you have brothers and sisters?
Non, **je** *n'*ai *qu'*un **frère.**	No, I only have one brother.

1. In simple tenses, *ne* precedes the verb, and *pas (plus, jamais,* etc.) follow the verb.

Je *ne* **veux** *pas* **ce livre.**	I don't want this book.
Il *ne* **vient** *jamais* **ici.**	He never comes here.

2. In perfect tenses, the second part of most negatives precedes the past participle.

Elle *n'*est *jamais* **montée à la Tour Eiffel.**	She never went to the top of the Eiffel Tower.

NOTE: *Personne, que,* and *aucun* follow the past participle.

Des lettres? *Non,* **il** *n'***a reçu** *aucune* **lettre.**	Letters? No, he received no letter.
Je *n'***ai invité** *personne* **pour ton anniversaire.**	I did not invite anyone for your birthday.

3. Both parts of a negative precede the infinitive.

Elle préfère *ne rien* **faire.**	She prefers to do nothing.
Il a fait semblant de *ne pas* **les voir.**	He pretended not to see them.

4. When the partitive is called for in a negative sentence, *pas de* replaces the partitive.

Tu as *du* **pain?** *Non,* **je** *n'***ai** *pas de* **pain.**	Do you have bread? No, I don't have bread.

5. *Ne. . .que* is the equivalent of "only" in French. *Que* comes before the word or words that are being restricted.

Ça *ne* **pouvait** *qu'***aggraver la situation.**	It could only have worsened the situation.

NOTE: When *seulement* ("only") is used to restrict the subject of a sentence, *ne* is omitted.

Seulement **lui aurait pu le faire.**	Only he could have done it.

6. *Rien, personne,* and *aucun* can also be used as subject pronouns. *Nul* is only used as a subject. In these cases, *ne* precedes the verb.

Rien ne **nous arrive jamais.**	Nothing ever happens to us.
*Personne n'***a parlé.**	No one spoke.
*Nul n'***est prophète en son pays.**	No one is a prophet in his own country.
Aucun **de ceux-là** *ne* **me plaît.**	None of these pleases me.

NOTE: The pronoun *personne* is masculine. The noun *personne* is feminine.

Personne ne **m'a parlé.**	No one spoke to me.
Il y avait deux *personnes* **qui étaient déjà arrivées.**	Two people had already arrived.

7. *Ni* precedes each word restricted by this negative.

Il *n'***y a** *ni* **sel** *ni* **poivre sur la table.**	There is neither salt nor pepper on the table.
Ils *n'***avaient** *ni* **faim** *ni* **soif.**	They were neither hungry nor thirsty.

8. In a few cases, *ne* is omitted. *Jamais* in this case takes the meaning of *ever.*

Plus **d'espoir!**	No more hope!
Auras-tu *jamais* **fini?**	Will you ever be finished?

NOTE: There are a few expressions or sayings in which *ne* is used without the second part of the negative.

*N'*importe!	No matter!
Si je *ne* me trompe. . .	If I am not mistaken. . .

NOTE: After *il y a, voilà,* or *voici* followed by a perfect tense, *ne* is often used alone.

Voilà longtemps que je *ne* t'ai vu.	It's been a long time since I saw you.

9. There are a few possible combinations of two or more negatives used with *ne.*

ne...plus guère	hardly ever	ne...jamais personne	never anyone
ne... plus personne	no one any more	ne...jamais rien	never anything
ne...plus rien	nothing any more	ne...jamais nulle part	nowhere any more
ne...plus jamais	never again	ne...jamais plus	never again

Je *ne* le vois *plus guère.*	I hardly ever see him.
Il *n'*y avait *plus personne.*	There was no one left any more.
Il *n'*y a *plus rien* à faire.	There is nothing left to do.
Tu *n'*invites *jamais personne.*	You never invite anyone.
Vous *ne* m'emmenez *jamais nulle part.*	You never take me anywhere.
Je *ne* le ferai *jamais plus.*	I will never do it again.
Je promets de *ne plus jamais* le faire.	I promise never to do it again.

10. *Ni. . .non plus* is used with nouns and emphatic pronouns.

Je n'en peux plus.	I can't go on any more.
Ni moi non plus.	Me neither.

Indefinite Pronouns

Indefinite pronouns, like indefinite adjectives (see page 70), refer either to something yet to be mentioned, or to something which has already been mentioned.

Tel est souvent pris qui croyait prendre.	He is often caught who thought he would be the one doing the catching.
Hélène et Jacqueline sont allées faire du ski. Pourtant, *l'une et l'autre* ont pris un train différent.	Helene and Jacqueline went skiing. Nevertheless, each took a different train.

Indefinite pronouns can be classed according to whether they are positive or negative in meaning.

Indefinite pronouns with a negative meaning

aucun(e) anyone, no one, nobody
nul no man, none
pas un(e) not one
personne nobody
rien nothing

NOTE: In sentences with these pronouns, *ne* must be used before the verb.

Rien *ne* **t'arrête.** Nothing is stopping you.
Personne *ne* **s'est trompé.** No one made a mistake.

Indefinite Pronouns with a positive meaning

These indefinite pronouns may refer to a unit, a group, or a whole.

> **on** one, we, they, people, etc.
> **l'un(e)...l'autre** the one...the other
> **un(e) autre** another
> **n'importe qui** anyone
> **n'importe quoi** anything
> **quelqu'un, quelqu'autre** someone, some other
> **quelque chose** something
> **quiconque** anyone
> **tel, un tel** such (person, thing), such a
> **le même** the same (person, thing)

As a group:

> **autrui** others, other people
> **les uns...les autres** the ones...the others
> **certains** some (people, animals, things)
> **plusieurs** several
> **plus d'un** more than one
> **la plupart** most of them
> **les mêmes** the same ones

As a whole:

> **chacun(e)** each one
> **tous** everyone
> **tout** all

NOTE: *On* may represent one or more persons. The corresponding possessive adjectives may be *son, sa,* or *ses.*

On **a** *ses* **habitudes.**	Each one of us has his own routine.
Ce n'est pas *n'importe qui.*	He is not just anyone.
—**A quoi penses-tu?** —A *quelque chose!*	—What are you thinking about? —Something!
Aucune **d'elles n'étaient jamais allée en Inde.**	None of them had ever been to India.
Les uns **parlaient,** *les autres* **écoutaient.**	Some were speaking, the others were listening.

NOTE: Indefinite adjectives were mentioned in the chapter dealing with adjectives (page 70). Many of them have the same form and meaning as the indefinite pronouns.

25. Prepositions

Like adverbs and conjunctions, prepositions are invariable. Prepositions are used to establish a rapport between two words or two groups of words in a sentence. They may precede nouns, verbs, adverbs, or phrases.

The Preposition À

1. The preposition *à* can follow a verb before an infinitive. (See the list of verbs that take *à* before an infinitive, Chapter 14.)

Chantal apprend *à* patiner.	Chantal is learning to skate.

2. *À* can be used to indicate place, time, or manner.

à droite	to the right	**à pied**	on foot
à loisir	at leisure	**à mort**	to death
à mon avis	in my opinion	**à la main**	handmade
à la campagne	in the country	**à la maison**	at home
à la française	(in) the French way	**à ce moment-là**	at that time

3. *À* can follow a verb before an indirect object.

Tu as donné cette viande *aux enfants*?	Did you give this meat to the children?
Non, je l'ai donnée *au chien*.	No, I gave it to the dog.

4. *À* can also be used to indicate possession.

Cette voiture est *à toi*?	This car is yours?
Non, elle est *à Christophe*.	No, it is Christophe's.

The Preposition *De*

1. *De* can come after a verb and before an infinitive. (See the list of verbs that take *de* before an infinitive, Chapter 14.)

Il s'arrête *de* courir.	He stops running.

NOTE: *De* is also used before an infinitive to become a predicate.

À vous *de* jouer!	Your turn to play!

2. *De* can be used to form an adverb.

de loin	from far away	**d'ici**	from here

3. *De* can also be used to form an adjective.

C'est tout ce qu'il y a *de plus* *vrai.*	It could not be more true.
Qu'est-ce que tu as fait *de beau?*	What did you do that was interesting?

4. *De* is also used to form a relation of time, point of view, cause, reason, or manner.

de l'heure	per hour	**d'instinct**	by instinct
de jour	by day	**de sang-froid**	in cold blood
de caractère	as for his (her) character	**de dépit**	in spite
		d'habitude	habitually

5. *De* may also be used to show possession. (See Chapter 18.)

C'est le tableau *de Nicole.*	That's Nicole's painting.

6. *De* also follows adverbs of quantity. (See Chapter 17.)

Julie a *beaucoup d'*argent.	Julie has a lot of money.

7. *De* comes after a noun that indicates quantity or measure or after a collective noun.

un litre *de* **lait**	a liter of milk
une paire *de* **bas**	a pair of stockings
une dizaine *de* **personnes**	about ten people
un million *de* **dollars**	one million dollars

NOTE: There is a difference in meaning between expressions using a noun + *à* and those using a noun + *de.*

un verre *de* **vin**	a glass of wine
un verre *à* **vin**	a wine glass
une tasse *de* **café**	a cup of coffee
une tasse *à* **café**	a coffee cup

8. *De* is used to express dimensions, to denote differences in age and measurement, and to denote English expressions of time.

La pièce a cinq mètres *de long.*	The room is five meters long.
Il est le plus âgé *de deux ans.*	He is older by two years.
Il est plus grand que Marc *de deux centimètres.*	He is two centimeters taller than Marc.
cinq heures *du matin*	5 A.M.
dix heures *du soir*	10 P.M.

9. *De* is also used in many adjective phrases.

un billet *de* **train**	a train ticket
un bureau *de* **tabac**	a tobacco store

10. *De* is used before the objects of some adjectives.

digne de foi	worthy of confidence
plein d'enthousiasme	full of enthusiasm
dur d'oreille	hard of hearing

À, *De,* and *En* with Place Names

To	à	cities	à Paris, à New York
	au, aux	countries (masculine), continents, provinces	au Portugal, aux États-Unis
	en	countries (feminine or beginning with a vowel or a mute *h*)	en Hollande, en Tunisie
From	de	cities, countries, continents, provinces (feminine or masculine beginning with a vowel or a mute *h*)	de Marseille, de Boston d'Allemagne
	de + *def. art.*	masculine countries, continents, provinces	du Québec, des Pays-Bas

Je vais *à* Beaune, *en* Bourgogne.	I am going to Beaune, in Burgundy.
Les Martin sont allés *au* Havre, *en* Normandie.	The Martins went to Le Havre, in Normandy.
Paul revient *du* Maroc. Il est allé *à* Marrakech.	Paul is coming back from Morocco. He went to Marrakesh.
Revenant d'un voyage *en* Italie et *au* Portugal, il est rentré fourbu *aux* États-Unis.	Coming back from a trip to Italy and Portugal, he came back exhausted to the States.

NOTE: When the place name is modified, *en* is replaced by *dans.*

Il va *en* Espagne.	He is going to Spain.
Il va *dans* l'Espagne de Don Quichotte.	He is going to the Spain of Don Quixote.

NOTE: When the idea of "inside" a city is conveyed, *dans* is used instead of *à.*

J'habite en plein *dans* Lyon.	I live in the center of Lyon.

NOTE: When place names are modified, *de* is replaced by *de la* or *du.*

Ils viennent *de la* belle province de Québec.	They come from the beautiful province of Quebec.
Nous aimons les quartiers *du* vieux Paris.	We love the districts of old Paris.

NOTE: Some cities contain an article in their names, which contract with *à* or *de.*

Mes parents reviennent *du* Caire. (Le Caire).	My parents are coming back from Cairo.

Other Uses of *En*

1. *En* can serve to form an adverb. (See Chapter 12.3, the formation of the gerund.)

Gérard entra *en* riant.	Gérard came in laughing.

2. *En* sometimes precedes a noun, a proper noun, an adjective, or a pronoun.

en soie	made of silk	**en juin**	in June
en laine	made of wool	**en été**	in summer
en noir	in black	**en voiture**	by car
en maths	in math	**en marche**	moving
en haut	upstairs	**en bois**	made of wood
en colère	angry	**en fête**	festive
en quoi	in what	**en qui**	in whom
croire en Dieu	to believe in God	**de fil en aiguille**	from thread to needle

3. *En* does not usually take an article after it, but both definite and indefinite articles are used in certain fixed expressions.

Il a dit ça *en l'air.*	He said that through his hat.
Nous buvons *en l'honneur de* **tes vingt ans.**	We are drinking in honor of your 20th birthday.
En ce temps-là, **nous étions plus heureux.**	At that time, we were happier.
J'aurai fini ça *en un mois.*	I'll have that finished in a month's time.

Other Prepositions

après after	**depuis** since, from	**jusque** up to, all the way to
d'après according to	**dès** at, as soon as	**parmi** among
auprès de close to	**devant** in front of	**sous** under
avant before	**pendant** during	**sur** on, over
avec with	**entre** between	**vers** toward
contre against	**envers** toward	
dans in, inside	**hors** out of	

Nous habitons là *depuis* **vingt ans.**	We have lived there for twenty years.
Ils suivirent la route *de* **Lyon,** *depuis* **Orléans** *jusqu'à* **Beaune.**	They followed the road to Lyon, from Orléans to Beaune.
Ils se dirigent *vers* **le jardin.**	They are going toward the garden.
Soyez gentils *envers* **votre frère.**	Be nice to your brother.

1. *Par* may be used in the sense of "by" (agent or means), "through," "out of," "in," or "on."

On est parti *par* **le train.**	We left by train.
Regarde *par* **la fenêtre!**	Look out the window!
Ne sors pas *par* **un temps pareil!**	Don't go out in such weather!
Nous nous voyons deux fois *par* **an.**	We see each other twice a year.

2. *Pour* may mean "for," "in place of," "among," "in the interest of," etc.

Ce gâteau est *pour* **mon filleul.**	This cake is for my godson.
Je répondrai *pour* **toi.**	I'll answer for you.
Mourir *pour* **son pays.**	To die for one's country.
Je ne fais rien *pour* **l'instant.**	I am doing nothing for the moment.
Nous partons demain *pour* **Berlin.**	We are leaving tomorrow for Berlin.
Elle est grande *pour* **une fille de son âge.**	She is tall for a girl her age.

26. Conjunctions

Conjunctions, like prepositions and adverbs, are invariable. Conjunctions connect two clauses, words, or group of words that have the same function in a sentence. There are two classes of conjunctions: conjunctions of coordination and conjunctions of subordination.

Conjunctions of Coordination

1. Liaison

et and
ensuite then
comme as
ni neither, nor

alors well, then
puis then
aussi also, thus

2. Cause

car since, because

en effet indeed

3. Consequence

donc thus
alors thus
par conséquent in consequence
de toute façon in any case

aussi thus
ainsi so
c'est pourquoi that's why

4. Transition

or now, then

5. Opposition

mais but
au contraire on the contrary
pourtant yet

et and
cependant however
d'ailleurs in any case

6. **ou** or

soit...soit either...or

7. **c'est à dire** that is

Ensuite, **ils sont tous allés au cinéma,** *car* **il faisait très mauvais. Mon père** *et* **ma mère, mon frère** *ou* **ma sœur, je ne me rappelle plus,** *mais* **pas moi.** *Donc,* **je suis resté tout seul à la maison.** *De toute façon,* **j'avais beaucoup de travail à faire.** *Alors,* **je ne me suis pas ennuyé.**

Then they all went to the movies, because the weather was terrible. My father and my mother, my brother or my sister, I don't remember, but not I. Thus, I stayed home by myself. Anyway, I had a lot of work to do. Well then, I did not get bored.

Conjunctions of Subordination

The conjunctions of subordination serve to connect a dependent clause to the main clause.

1. Cause

comme as
parce que because

puisque since
d'autant que as far as

2. Consequence

que (+ *subj.*) that
si bien que so that

de sorte que so that

3. Goal

afin que in order that
tellement que so much that

pour que so that
de peur que for fear that

4. Concession, opposition

bien que though, although
quoique although
alors que when

quand même just the same
malgré que in spite of the fact that
sans que without (gerund)

Janine s'est acheté un nouveau chapeau, *bien qu*'**elle en ait des douzaines.**

Janine bought a new hat, even though she has dozens of them.

Il n'ose pas sortir *de peur que* **le vent ne le décoiffe.**

He does not dare go out, for fear that the wind will undo his hairdo.

Je veux pourtant qu'il sorte, *parce qu*'**il ne prend jamais l'air.**

I want him to go out, however, because he never gets fresh air.

27. Time

Days of the Week

lundi   Monday
mardi   Tuesday
mercredi   Wednesday
jeudi   Thursday
vendredi   Friday
samedi   Saturday
dimanche   Sunday

The days of the week are all masculine and are not capitalized. They are not usually preceded by a definite article, unless it is to express a repeated occurrence.

Aujourd'hui, c'est lundi.	Today is Monday.
Je travaille *le* **samedi.**	I work on Saturdays.
Mardi prochain, j'irai au cinéma.	Next Tuesday, I'll go to the movies.
À jeudi!	See you Thursday!

Months of the Year

janvier   January
février   February
mars   March
avril   April
mai   May
juin   June

juillet   July
août   August
septembre   September
octobre   October
novembre   November
décembre   December

The months of the year are masculine and are not capitalized.

Seasons of the Year

le printemps   spring
l'été (*m.*)   summer

l'automne (*m.*)   fall, autumn
l'hiver (*m.*)   winter

The Date

The ordinal *premier* is used for the first of each month. For all other dates the cardinal numbers are used.

Nous sommes le combien aujourd'hui?	
C'est le combien aujourd'hui?	What is the date?
Quelle date sommes-nous?	
C'est le premier mai.	It is the first of May.
C'est le deux mai. Le deux.	It's the second of May. The second.
Nous sommes le premier juin.	It's the first of June.
Nous sommes le vingt-trois juin.	It is the twenty-third of June.
Le vingt-trois.	The twenty-third.

The French write the date in the following manner: *le 5 avril 1983*

day | month | year
5 / 4 / 83 = le 5 avril 1983

Divisions of Time

la seconde	second	**la nuit**	night
la minute	minute	**le jour, la journée**	day
l'heure (*f.*)	hour	**la semaine**	week
la demi-heure	half an hour	**le mois**	month
le quart d'heure	a quarter of an hour	**la saison**	season
le matin, la matinée	morning	**l'an** (*m.*) **l'année** (*f.*)	year
l'après-midi (*f.*)	afternoon	**le siècle**	century
le soir, la soirée	evening		

NOTE: *Le matin, le soir, le jour,* and *l'an* are used when talking about a precise time; *la matinée, la soirée, la journée,* and *l'année* indicate a duration of time.

J'ai passé *un an* **à Paris.**	I spent a year in Paris.
Je n'ai rien fait de *toute l'année.*	I did nothing all year.
Passez dans *la matinée.*	Come sometime in the morning.

Expressions of Time

naintenant now	**demain matin** tomorrow morning
out de suite right now	**hier après-midi** yesterday afternoon
iujourd'hui today	**la semaine dernière** last week
:e matin this morning	**la semaine prochaine** next week
:e soir tonight	**toute la journée** all day
:et après-midi this afternoon	**tous les jours** every day
iier yesterday	**tout le temps** all the time
lemain tomorrow	**au début du mois** at the beginning of the month
ivant-hier the day before yesterday	**au milieu de la semaine** about the middle of the week
iprès-demain the day after tomorrow	**à la fin de l'année** at the end of the year
e matin in the morning	**quelque temps** sometime
'après-midi in the afternoon	**quelques jours** a few days
e soir in the evening	**à la mi-septembre** about mid-september
a nuit at night	**vers neuf heures** about nine o'clock

Time of Day

Quelle heure est-il?	What time is it?
Il est une heure.	It is one o'clock.
Il est deux heures.	It is two o'clock.
Il est midi.	It is noon.
Il est minuit.	It is midnight.
À quelle heure?	At what time?
À cinq heures (juste).	At five o'clock (sharp).
À six heures cinq.	At five past six.
À sept heures et quart.	At quarter past seven.
À huit heures et demie.	At eight-thirty.
À midi et demi.	At half past noon.
À dix heures moins le quart.	At quarter to ten.
À vingt-et-une heures quarante cinq.	At quarter to ten (P.M.) (9:45).
À onze heures moins dix.	At ten to eleven.
À vingt-deux heures cinquante.	At ten to eleven (P.M.) (10:50).

NOTE: The 24-hour clock is used in France for train, plane, bus, and theater schedules, and often for appointments.

22 heures = 10:00 P.M.

NOTE: *Demi* is masculine in the expressions *midi et demi* and *minuit et demi,* while *demie* agrees with *heure (f.)* in all other cases.

The Cardinal Points

le nord	north	le nord-est	northeast
le sud	south	le sud-est	southeast
l'est (*m.*)	east	le nord-ouest	northwest
l'ouest (*m.*)	west	le sud-ouest	southwest

28. Numbers and Units of Measurement

Cardinal Numbers

0 zéro	21 vingt et un	76 soixante-seize
1 un, une	22 vingt-deux	77 soixante-dix-sept
2 deux	23 vingt-trois	78 soixante-dix-huit
3 trois	24 vingt-quatre	79 soixante-dix-neuf
4 quatre	25 vingt-cinq	80 quatre-vingts
5 cinq	26 vingt-six	81 quatre-vingt-un
6 six	27 vingt-sept	90 quatre-vingt-dix
7 sept	28 vingt-huit	91 quatre-vingt-onze
8 huit	29 vingt-neuf	100 cent
9 neuf	30 trente	101 cent un
10 dix	31 trente et un	200 deux cents
11 onze	32 trente-deux	300 trois cents
12 douze	40 quarante	400 quatre cents
13 treize	50 cinquante	500 cinq cents
14 quatorze	60 soixante	600 six cents
15 quinze	70 soixante-dix	700 sept cents
16 seize	71 soixante et onze	800 huit cents
17 dix-sept	72 soixante-douze	900 neuf cents
18 dix-huit	73 soixante-treize	1000 mille
19 dix-neuf	74 soixante-quatorze	2000 deux mille
20 vingt	75 soixante-quinze	1.000.000 un million (de)
		1.000.000.000 un milliard

The plural -s is required after *cent* in even hundreds like *deux cents,* but is dropped when *cent* is followed by another number.

265   **deux cent soixante-cinq**

Above a thousand, numbers and dates can be read in thousands or in hundreds. *Mille* is often shortened to *mil.*

1983   **mil neuf cent quatre-vingt-trois**
dix-neuf cent quatre-vingt-trois

Note also that a period or a blank is used in figures 1.000 and above; a comma is used to mark the division between whole numbers and decimals.

10 245   **10.245**   **27,50**

Other remarks: *Un* is used when counting and with masculine nouns; *une* is used with feminine nouns.

Odd and even numbers:

impair odd
pair even

de deux en deux by two's
de dix en dix by ten's

Les numéros impairs sont 3, 5, 7, etc.
The odd numbers are 3, 5, 7, etc.

Les numéros pairs sont 2, 4, 6, etc.
The even numbers are 2, 4, 6, etc.

Comptez de cinq en cinq, de cinq à cinquante.
Count by five's from five to fifty.

Collective Numbers

la paire (de) two, a pair of
la dizaine (de) ten, about ten
la douzaine (de) a dozen
la quinzaine (de) fifteen, about fifteen
la vingtaine (de) twenty

la centaine (de) hundred
le millier (de) thousand
le million (de) million
le milliard (de) billion

Ordinal Numbers

1st	**premier, première**	17th	**dix-septième**
2nd	**deuxième, second(e)**	18th	**dix-huitième**
3rd	**troisième**	19th	**dix-neuvième**
4th	**quatrième**	20th	**vingtième**
5th	**cinquième**	21st	**vingt et unième**
6th	**sixième**	22nd	**vingt-deuxième**
7th	**septième**	30th	**trentième**
8th	**huitième**	40th	**quarantième**
9th	**neuvième**	50th	**cinquantième**
10th	**dixième**	60th	**soixantième**
11th	**onzième**	70th	**soixante-dixième**
12th	**douzième**	80th	**quatre-vingtième**
13th	**treizième**	90th	**quatre-vingt-dixième**
14th	**quatorzième**	100th	**centième**
15th	**quinzième**	1000th	**millième**
16th	**seizième**	1,000,000th	**millionième**

Ordinals may be abbreviated by using a figure and adding *-ème.* 1st adds *-er* or *-ère,* depending on the gender of the noun to which it refers. Ordinals precede the noun.

22ème **le vingt-deuxième étage**
the twenty-third floor
1ère **la première page**
the first page

Fractions

1/2 demi(e) (*adj.*) la moitié (*noun*)	1/6 un sixième	1/12 un douzième
	1/7 un septième	1/13 un treizième
1/3 un tiers	1/8 un huitième	1/14 un quatorzième
1/4 un quart	1/9 un neuvième	1/20 un vingtième
3/4 trois-quart	1/10 un dixième	1/100 un centième
1/5 un cinquième	1/11 un onzième	1/1000 un millième
	% pour cent	

Demi ("half") is an adjective and agrees in gender with the noun to which it refers.

une heure et demie   one o'clock

Demi is invariable when followed by a hyphen.

une demi-livre de sucre   half pound of sugar

La moitié ("half") is a noun.

J'ai mangé la moitié de la pomme.   I have eaten half of the apple.
La moitié de 4 est 2.   Half of 4 is 2.

Decimals

la décimale   tenth, decimal   **le centésimal**   hundredth

Arithmetical Signs

+ et, plus	addition	$2 + 2 = 4$	Deux plus deux font quatre.
− moins	soustraction	$8 - 7 = 1$	Huit moins sept font un.
× multiplié par	multiplication	$2 \times 3 = 6$	Deux multiplié par trois font six.
÷ divisé par	division	$6 \div 3 = 2$	Six divisé par trois font deux.

additionner   to add   **multiplier**   to multiply
soustraire   to subtract   **diviser**   to divide

Dimensions

Nouns	Adjectives
la hauteur height	**haut,-e** high, tall
la longueur length	**long, longue** long
la largeur width	**large** wide
la profondeur depth	**profond,-e** deep
l'épaisseur (*f.*) thickness	**épais,-se** thick

Avoir is often used to express dimensions.

La Tour Eiffel a trois cents mètres de haut.	The Eiffel Tower is 300 meters high.
La Loire a mille douze kilomètres de long.	The Loire river is 1,012 kilometers long.
Ce bifteck a trois centimètres d'épaisseur.	This steak is 3 centimeters thick.

Être de is also used to express dimensions.

La profondeur de ce puits est de trente mètres.	The depth of this well is 30 meters.
La largeur de ce paquet est de 75 centimètres.	The width of this package is 75 centimeters.

To tell someone's height, the verb *mesurer* is used. *Faire* can also be used.

Marc mesure un mètre quatre-vingt.	Marc is 1 m. 80 tall.
Ce meuble fait bien trois mètres.	This piece of furniture is at least three meters high.

Units of Measure, Metric System

l'hectare (*m.*)	hectare	(about 2 1/2 acres)
le kilo (kilogramme)	kilogram	(2.2 pounds)
le mètre	meter	(39.37 inches)
le kilomètre	kilometer	(about 5/8 of a mile)
le centimètre	centimeter	(0.39 inches)
le litre	liter	(a little over a quart)
la tonne	ton	(200 kilos)

Other Units of Measurement

le pouce	inch	**la pinte**	pint
le pied	foot	**le gallon**	gallon
le yard	yard	**la livre**	pound
le mille	mile		

Geometrical Terms

Surfaces planes:

la ligne	line	**le rectangle**	rectangle
l'angle (*m.*)	angle	**l'hexagone** (*m.*)	hexagon
l'angle droit (*m.*)	right angle	**le cercle**	circle
le triangle	triangle	**le diamètre**	diameter
le carré	square	**le rayon**	radius

Solids:

le cube cube	**la pyramide** pyramid
le cylindre cylinder	**le cône** cone
la sphère sphere	**le prisme** prism
l'hémisphère (*m.*) hemisphere	

29. Letters

Parts of a Letter

l'en-tête(*m.*)   heading
la vedette   name and address
l'appel (*m.*)   salutation
la date   date
l'objet (*m.*)   subject
le corps de la lettre   body of the letter
la référence   reference
la signature   signature

la formule de salutations   salutation (end)
la pièce jointe (P.J.) (pièces jointes)   enclosures
le code postal   zip code
CEDEX (Courrier d'entreprise à Distribution Exceptionnelle)   Business M
Boîte Postale   P.O. box

Heading

Lyon, le 5 avril 1983
New York, le 1er janvier 1983

Dakar, le 6 juin 1984
Montréal, le 30 septembre 1984

Address

Madame Solange Delhorme
6, rue Vendôme
22000 Grenoble
France

Monsieur le Directeur
Peugeot S.A.
58, avenue Général de Gaulle
69002 Lyon   France

Salutations

Business Letters

Monsieur, Sir:, Dear Sir:
Messieurs, Sirs:, Dear Sirs:
Madame et chère cliente,
   Madam and dear customer:

For more formal letters

Monsieur le Président, Mr. President:
Cher Maître, (to a lawyer or a notary)
Madame la Directrice,
   (to a woman director)

NOTE: One uses *cher (chère)* only when one knows the person well. When you do not know whether the woman is married or not, use *Madame*.

Personal letters

Cher ami, Chère amie,
Cher Paul, Chère Virginie
Mon cher cousin, Ma chère cousine
Ma chère petite Brigitte,

Dear friend,
Dear Paul, Dear Virginia,
Dear cousin,
Dear little Brigitte,

Ending

Formal or business letters

Je vous prie d'agréer (Veuillez recevoir), monsieur (madame, mademoiselle), l'expression de mes (nos) sentiments dévoués (distingués, respecteux).

Literally: Please accept, Sir (Madam, Miss, or Ms.), the expression of my (our) devoted (distinguished, respectful) sentiments.

Personal letters

Amitiés   With friendship,
Affectueusement,   Affectionately,
Ton copain,   Your pal,
Ton amie,   Your friend,
Bons baisers,   Affectionate kisses,
Je t'embrasse,   I kiss you,
A bientôt le plaisir de te lire   I hope to have the pleasure soon
  (voir, parler)   to hear from (see, speak to) you.

Abbreviations

M.	monsieur	Mr.
Mme	madame	Mrs.
Mlle	mademoiselle	Miss or Ms.
MM.	messieurs	gentlemen, sirs
C.V.	curriculum vitae	résumé
C.C.P.	Compte chèque postal	postal bank account
Cie	compagnie	company
c.c.	copie conforme	carbon copy
P.J.	pièces jointes	enclosures
P.S.	postscriptum	postscript (P.S.)
P.-D.G.	Président-directeur général	Chairman and president
P.T.T.	Postes, télégraphes et téléphone	Postal, telegraph and telephone services
S.A.	société anonyme	incorporated company
S.A.R.L.	société anonyme à responsabilité limitée	limited liability company
R.S.V.P.	réponse, s'il vous plaît	please reply
	retournez, s'il vous plaît	please return
Ref.	Références	references
S.V.P.	s'il vous plaît	please

30. Idioms and Expressions

A

à bas. . .! down with . . .!
à bientôt see you soon
d'abord at first
à cause de because of
d'accord agreed, OK
à droite to the right
à l'envers inside out
à la française the French way
à gauche to the left
à l'heure on time
à la légère lightly
à la longue in the long run
à la maison at home
à la mode in fashion
à mi-temps part-time
à nouveau again
à part aside
à peine hardly
à plein temps full-time
à peu près nearly, approximately
à temps on time
à tort ou à raison rightly or wrongly
A vos souhaits! God bless you!
aller bien to be well
aller chez soi to go home
aller mal to not feel well
aller mieux to feel better
Allons-y! Let's go!
allumer la télé to turn on the TV
au courant (de) informed (about)
avoir l'air (de) + *inf* to seem to
avoir l'air (de) + *noun* to look like
avoir. . .ans to be. . .years old
avoir besoin (de) to need
avoir de la chance to be lucky
avoir chaud to be warm, hot
avoir confiance en to have confidence in
avoir envie (de) to want
avoir faim to be hungry
avoir froid to be cold
avoir hâte (de) to be anxious to
avoir l'intention (de) to intend
avoir lieu to take place
avoir mal to hurt
avoir le mal du pays to be homesick

en avoir marre to be fed up
avoir de la peine to suffer, to be hurt
avoir peur (de) to be afraid (of)
avoir raison to be right
avoir soif to be thirsty
avoir sommeil to be sleepy
avoir tort to be wrong
à voix basse softly
à voix haute loudly

B

bas:en bas downstairs
bien de a lot of
bien des many
bien sûr! of course!
bienvenue! welcome!
bon anniversaire! happy birthday!
bon courage! have courage!
bon marché inexpensive, reasonably priced
bonne année! happy New Year!
bonne chance! good luck!

C

chic, alors! great!
ci-inclus enclosed
ci-joint enclosed
Comment ça se fait? How come?
s'y connaître to be an expert in, to know all about
contre: par contre on the other hand
le coucher du soleil sundown
le coup de chance stroke of luck
le coup de fil telephone call
le coup d'œil glance

D

se débrouiller to manage, to work things out
défense de. . . it's forbidden to. . .
depuis longtemps for a long time
dieu: mon dieu! good heavens!
dire du mal (de) to talk ill (of)
dis donc! say!
donner à manger to feed
se donner du mal to go out of one's way

E

l'emploi du temps   schedule
en face de   opposite
en marche   in motion
entendre dire (que)   to hear (that)
entendre parler (de)   to hear (of)
entendu!   all right!
être de bonne humeur   to be in a good mood
être en train (de)   to be doing (something)
exemple: par exemple   for example

F

faire: s'en faire   to worry
faire attention   to be careful, to pay attention
faire de l'autostop   to hitchhike
faire du bricolage   to putter, to tinker
faire comme chez soi   to feel at home
faire confiance à   to trust (someone)
faire des courses   to go shopping
faire la cuisine   to cook
faire faire   to have something done
faire la lessive   to do the laundry
se faire mal   to get hurt
faire mal (à)   to hurt someone (physically)
faire sa médecine (son droit)   to study medicine (law)
faire le ménage   to do housework
faire de la peine (à)   to hurt someone's feelings
faire peur   to frighten
faire une promenade   to take a walk
faire la queue   to stand in line
faire réparer   to have (something) repaired
faire le repassage   to do the ironing
faire semblant (de)   to pretend (to)
faire du sport   to go in for sports
faire la vaisselle   to do the dishes
faire venir   to send for
faire un voyage   to take a trip
faute: sans faute   without fail
ficher: s'en ficher   not to care
fois: deux fois   twice
fois: pour la première fois   for the first time
fois: une fois   once
faut: comme il faut   properly
faut: ce qu'il te (vous) faut   what you need

G

grâce à   thanks to

H

d'habitude   usually, habitually
hasard: par hasard   by chance
haut: en haut   upstairs

I

ici: par ici   this way
n'importe   no matter
n'importe comment   no matter how
n'importe où   no matter where
n'importe quand   no matter when
n'importe qui   no matter who
n'importe quoi   no matter what
à l'instant   immediately, a moment ago

J

jeter un coup d'œil (sur)   to glance (at)
jouer à   to play (a sport)
jouer de   to play (a musical instrument)
le jour de congé   day off
jusqu'à   up to, as far as

L

là-bas   over there
le lever du soleil   sunrise

M

la machine à calculer   calculator
la machine à coudre   sewing machine
la machine à laver le linge   washing machine
manquer de (+ *noun*)   to be missing, to lack
manquer de (+ *inf.*)   to fail to, to come near to
marcher bien   to be in good order
marcher mal   to be out of condition
mettre de côté   to put aside, to save
mettre la table   to set the table
mettre la radio   to turn on the radio
mieux vaut   it's better to
mourir de faim   to starve
mourir de rire   to die laughing

N

n'est-ce pas?   is it not so?

O

l'offre d'emploi (*m.*) want ad
ouf! exclamation of relief

P

en panne out of order
se passer de to live without
passer le temps to spend time
peu importe never mind
pouvoir: n'en pouvoir plus to be exhausted
prendre soin de to take care of
prendre son temps to take one's time
prière de (verbe) please (verb)

Q

quand même even so, just the same
Qu'est-ce que c'est? What is it?
Qu'est-ce qui arrive? What's happening?
Qu'est-ce qu'il y a? What's the matter?
Qu'est-ce qui se passe? What is happening?
Qu'est-ce qui s'est passé? What happened?
Qu'est-ce qu'il te prend? What has come over you?
Quelle barbe! What a bore!

R

se rendre compte de/que to take into account, to realize
en retard late

S

sain et sauf safe and sound
sens: le bon sens common sense
sens dessus dessous upside down
se sentir bien to feel well
serrer la main to shake hands
tout(e) seul(e) all alone
sortir: s'en sortir to pull through, to get by

suivre un conseil to follow advice
suivre un cours to take a course

T

tant de so many, so much
tel quel just as it is, in the same condition
de temps en temps from time to time
tenir à to insist, to be bent on doing something
tenir compte de to take into account
tenir de to take after, resemble
tiens! why! well! look here!
tout à l'heure a little later
tout d'abord first of all
tout droit straight ahead
tout d'un coup all of a sudden
tous les deux the two of us, together
tout le monde everybody
tout près (de) very close (to)

U

l'un d'entre eux one of them
d'urgence urgently, immediately

V

vacances: les grandes vacances summer vacation
valoir le coup to be worthwhile
valoir mieux to be better
valoir la peine to be worthwhile, to be worth the trouble
vive. . .! long live. . .!
vouloir dire to mean
en vouloir à to have a grudge against, be resentful

Y

y compris included

Z

zut, alors! darn!

31. Vocabulary Lists

French-Speaking Countries

le pays	country	la capitale	capital
la France	France	Paris	Paris
la Belgique	Belgium	Bruxelles	Brussels
le Canada (Québec)	Canada (Quebec)	Québec	Quebec (capital of province of Quebec)
le Luxembourg	Luxembourg	Luxembourg	Luxembourg
la Suisse	Switzerland	Berne	Bern

Les Départements d'outre-mer ("DOM's")

(Overseas departments, having the same status as a department in France.)

le département	political division of France	la préfecture capital of department
la Guadeloupe	Guadeloupe	Pointe-à-Pître
la Guyane française	French Guyana	Cayenne
la Martinique	Martinique	Fort-de-France
Saint-Martin	French Saint-Martin	Philipsburg

Les Territoires d'outre-mer

(Overseas territories)

le territoire	territory	la capitale	capital
la Nouvelle-Calédonie	New Caledonia	Nouméa	
la Polynésie	French Polynesia	Papeete	
la Réunion	Reunion	Saint-Denis	

Countries Where French Is Spoken as an Official Language

Pays		Capitale
le Bénin	Benin	Porto-Novo
le Burundi	Burundi	Usumbura
le Cameroun	Cameroon	Yaoundé
le Congo	Congo	Brazzaville
la Côte d'Ivoire	Ivory Coast	Abidjan
le Gabon	Gabon	Libreville
la Guinée	Guinea	Conakry
Haïti	Haiti	Port-au-Prince
la Haute-Volta	Upper Volta	Ouagadougou
le Laos	Laos	Vientiane
Madagascar	Madagascar	Tananarive

le Mali	Mali	**Bamako**
la Mauritanie	Mauritania	**Nouakchott**
le Niger	Niger	**Niamey**
la République Centrafricaine	Central African Republic	**Bangui**
la Ruanda	Rwanda	**Kigali**
le Sénégal	Senegal	**Dakar**
le Tchad	Chad	**Ndjamena**
le Togo	Togo	**Lomé**
la Zaïre	Zaire	**Kinshasa**

Countries Where French Is Spoken as a Second Language

l'Algérie	Algeria	**Alger**
le Maroc	Morocco	**Rabat**
la Tunisie	Tunisia	**Tunis**

Commonly Used Words and Phrases

Current Expressions

Bonjour! Good morning! Good day!
Bonsoir! Good evening!
Bonne nuit! Good night!
Salut! Hi!
Comment allez-vous? How are you?
Comment vas-tu? How are you?
Ça va? Ça va. How's it going? OK.
Bien, très bien. Well, very well.
Pas mal, merci. Not bad, thank you.
Au revoir! Good-bye!
A bientôt! See you soon!
A demain! See you tomorrow!
A lundi! See you Monday!
D'accord! OK!

monsieur Mr., sir
madame Mrs., lady
mademoiselle Miss, Ms., young lady
Oui, madame! Yes, ma'am!
Non, monsieur! No, sir!
s'il vous plaît please
Merci beaucoup! Thank you very much!
Je vous en prie.
De rien. } You're welcome.
Il n'y a pas de quoi.
Excusez-moi. Excuse me, I'm sorry.
Je m'excuse. I'm sorry.
Pardon. I beg your pardon.

Nationalities and Languages

allemand — l'allemand (*m.*) German
anglais — l'anglais (*m.*) English
chinois — le chinois Chinese
espagnol — l'espagnol (*m.*) Spanish
français — le français French
italien — l'italien (*m.*) Italian
japonais — le japonais Japanese
portugais — le portugais Portuguese
russe — le russe Russian

Commonly Used Items

le cahier (d'exercices) notebook (workbook)
la carte map
la corbeille à papiers wastepaper basket
la craie chalk
le crayon pencil
l'encre (*f.*) ink
l'enveloppe (*f.*) envelope
l'examen (*m.*) exam, test
la gomme eraser
la lettre letter
le livre book
le papier paper
le stylo pen
le tableau chalkboard
le timbre stamp

Beverages

la bière beer
la boisson drink, beverage
le café coffee
le café crème coffee with cream

le **chocolat**   hot chocolate
le **cidre**   cider
l'**eau** (*f.*)   water
l'**eau minérale** (*f.*)   mineral water
la **glace**   ice
le **jus d'orange**   orange juice
le **jus de pamplemousse**   grapefruit
   juice
le **lait**   milk
la **limonade**   lemon soda
le **thé**   tea
le **vin**   wine

Food

les **aliments** (*m.*)   food
le **beurre**   butter
le **biscuit**   cracker
le **bonbon**   candy
les **conserves** (*f.*)   canned goods
le **croissant**   crescent roll
le **fromage**   cheese
le **gâteau**   cake
la **glace**   ice cream
l'**huile** (*f.*)   oil
le **macaroni**   macaroni
le **miel**   honey
la **moutarde**   mustard
la **nouille**   noodle
le **pain**   bread
le **pâté**   pâté
le **pâté de foie gras**   goose liver pâté
le **petit gâteau**   cookie
le **petit pain**   roll
le **poivre**   pepper
le **riz**   rice
le **sandwich**   sandwich
le **sel**   salt
le **spaghetti**   spaghetti
le **sucre**   sugar
la **tarte**   pie
le **vinaigre**   vinegar

Meats

l'**agneau** (*m.*)   lamb
le **bifteck**   steak
le **bœuf**   beef
la **côtelette**   cutlet, chop
l'**escalope** (*f.*)   cutlet
le **foie**   liver
le **gigot**   leg of lamb
le **jambon**   ham
le **lard**   bacon
le **mouton**   lamb
le **porc**   pork

le **rognon**   kidney
le **rosbif**   roast beef
la **saucisse**   sausage
le **saucisson**   salami
le **veau**   veal

Fowl

le **canard**   duck
la **dinde**   turkey
l'**oie** (*f.*)   goose
le **poulet**   chicken
la **volaille**   fowl

Fish

la **crevette**   shrimp
l'**huître** (*f.*)   oyster
la **langouste**   lobster
la **morue**   cod
la **moule**   mussel
la **palourde**   clam
le **poisson**   fish
la **sardine**   sardine
le **saumon**   salmon
le **thon**   tuna
la **truite**   trout

Vegetables

l'**ail** (*m.*)   garlic
l'**artichaut** (*m.*)   artichoke
l'**asperge** (*f.*)   asparagus
la **carotte**   carrot
le **céleri**   celery
le **chou**   cabbage
le **chou-fleur**   cauliflower
l'**épinard** (*m.*)   spinach
le **haricot vert**   green bean
la **laitue**   lettuce
le **légume**   vegetable
le **maïs**   corn
l'**oignon** (*m.*)   onion
l'**olive** (*f.*)   olive
le **persil**   parsley
le **petit pois**   pea
le **poireau**   leek
le **poivron**   pepper
la **pomme de terre**   potato
le **radis**   radish
la **tomate**   tomato

Fruits and Nuts

l'**abricot** (*m.*)   apricot
l'**airelle** (*f.*)   cranberry

l'amande (*f.*) almond
l'ananas (*m.*) pineapple
l'avocat (*m.*) avocado
la **banane** banana
la **cacahuète** peanut
la **cerise** cherry
le **citron** lemon
la **date** date
la **figue** fig
la **fraise** strawberry
la **framboise** raspberry
le **fruit** fruit
le **melon** melon, cantaloupe
la **mûre** blackberry
la **myrtille** blueberry
la **noisette** hazelnut
la **noix** walnut
l'orange (*f.*) orange
le **pamplemousse** grapefruit
la **pastèque** watermelon
la **pêche** peach
la **poire** pear
la **pomme** apple
la **prune** plum
le **raisin** grape

Meals

le **casse-croûte** heavy snack
le **déjeuner** lunch (midday meal)
le **dîner** dinner (evening meal)
le **goûter** afternoon snack (for children)
le **petit déjeuner** breakfast
le **pique-nique** picnic
le **repas** meal
le **souper** supper (late evening)

Menu

la **(sauce) béarnaise** hot sauce with butter, egg yolks, shallots, and tarragon
la **bouillabaisse** fish soup
le **civet de lapin** rabbit stew
le **croûton** crouton
le **dessert** dessert
l'entrée (*f.*) first course
les **escargots** (*m.*) snails
les **fruits de mer** (*m.*) seafood
la **(sauce) hollandaise** hot sauce with butter, egg yolks, and lemon
le **hors d'œuvre** hors d'oeuvre
la **mayonnaise** mayonnaise

la **note** check (in restaurant)
l'œuf dur (*m.*) hard-boiled egg
l'omelette (*f.*) omelet
le **plat du jour** the special (of the day)
le **plateau de fromages** cheese tray
le **potage** thick soup
le **pourboire** tip
la **quiche** quiche
le **ragoût** meat stew
le **rôti** roast
la **salade** salad
la **sauce (de salade)** dressing
la **soupe** soup
la **vinaigrette** dressing of mustard, vinegar, and oil

bleu rare
saignant medium rare
à point well done
à la carte separate price for each dish
au jus with natural juices
au gratin broiled with topping of cheese
en brochette on a skewer
en croûte in a pastry shell
en purée mashed
le **cordon bleu** excellent cook
le **chef de cuisine** chef

The Table

l'assiette (*f.*) plate
la **cafetière** coffeepot
la **corbeille à pain** breadbasket
le **couteau** knife
la **cuillère (à soupe)** (soup)spoon
la **fourchette** fork
la **nappe** tablecloth
le **plat** (serving) dish
le **plateau** tray
le **poivrier** pepper mill
la **salière** saltshaker
le **sucrier** sugar bowl
la **théière** teapot
la **vaisselle** dishes
le **verre** glass

mettre le couvert to set the table
débarrasser la table to clear the table

The Human Body

la **barbe** beard
la **bouche** mouth

le bras   arm
les cheveux (*m.*)   hair
la cheville   ankle
le cil   eyelash
le cœur   heart
le coude   elbow
la dent   tooth
le doigt   finger
le doigt de pied   toe
le dos   back
l'épaule (*f.*)   shoulder
l'estomac (*m.*)   stomach
la figure   face
le foie   liver
le front   forehead
le genou   knee
la gorge   throat
la jambe   leg
la joue   cheek
la langue   tongue
la lèvre   lip
la main   hand
le menton   chin
la moustache   mustache
le nez   nose
l'œil (*m.*) (les yeux)   eye
l'ongle (*m.*)   nail
l'oreille (*f.*)   ear
la paupière   eyelid
la peau   skin
le pied   foot
le poignet   wrist
la poitrine   chest
le sourcil   eyebrow
la tête   head
le visage   face

The Family and Relatives

l'arrière-grand-mère (*f.*)   great-
   grandmother
l'arrière-grand-père (*m.*)   great-
   grandfather
le beau-fils   stepson
le beau-frère   brother-in-law
le beau-père   father-in-law, stepfather
la belle-fille   stepdaughter, daughter-
   in-law
la belle-mère   mother-in-law,
   stepmother
la belle-sœur   sister-in-law
la bru   daughter-in-law
le cousin, la cousine   cousin
l'enfant (*m. & f.*)   child

l'époux, l'épouse   spouse
la famille   family
la femme   wife
la fille   daughter
le fils   son
le frère   brother
le gendre   son-in-law
la grand-mère   grandmother
le grand-père   grandfather
le mari   husband
la mère   mother
le neveu   nephew
la nièce   niece
l'oncle (*m.*)   uncle
les parents (*m.*)   parents, relatives
le père   father
la petite-fille   granddaughter
le petit-fils   grandson
les petits-enfants (*m.*)   grandchildren
la sœur   sister
la tante   aunt

The House

l'appartement (*m.*)   apartment
l'ascenseur (*m.*)   elevator
la chambre   bedroom
la cheminée   chimney, fireplace
le corridor   corridor
la cuisine   kitchen
l'entrée (*f.*)   foyer
l'escalier (*m.*)   stairs
la fenêtre   window
le gratte-ciel   skyscraper
l'immeuble (*m.*)   apartment building
la maison   house
le mur   wall
la pièce   room
le placard   closet, cupboard
le plafond   ceiling
le plancher   floor
la porte-fenêtre   French window
le premier (étage)   second floor
le rez-de-chaussée   first (main) floor
la salle à manger   dining room
la salle de bains   bathroom
la salle de séjour   combination living
   and dining room
le salon   living room
le toit   roof

Furniture

l'armoire (*f.*)   wardrobe

le buffet   china cabinet
le bureau   desk
la chaise   chair
la commode   dresser
la cuisinière   stove
le fauteuil   armchair
la lampe   lamp
le lit   bed
le lustre   chandelier
le meuble   furniture
la moquette   carpeting
le réfrigérateur   refrigerator
le rideau   curtain
la table   table
le tableau   painting
le tapis   rug

The Bed

faire le lit   to make the bed
la couverture   blanket
le dessus-de-lit   bedspread
le drap   sheet
l'édredon (*m.*)   comforter
le matelas   mattress
l'oreiller (*m.*)   pillow
la taie d'oreiller   pillowcase

Toilet Articles

la brosse   brush
la brosse à dents   toothbrush
les ciseaux   scissors
la crème à raser   shaving cream
la crème solaire   suntan lotion
le dentifrice   toothpaste
l'eau de Cologne (*f.*)   cologne
la lime à ongles   nail file
le miroir   mirror
le parfum   perfume
le peigne   comb
la poudre   powder
le rasoir   razor
le rouge à lèvres   lipstick
le savon   soap
la serviette de toilette   towel
le shampooing   shampoo

Clothing

la blouse   blouse
le blouson   windbreaker
la ceinture   belt
le chapeau   hat

la chaussette   sock
la chaussure   shoe
la chemise   shirt
le col   collar
le collant   pantyhose
le complet   suit
la cravate   necktie
le gant   glove
l'imperméable (*m.*)   raincoat
le jean   jeans
la jupe   skirt
la lingerie   lingerie
le manteau   coat
la mode   fashion
le mouchoir   handkerchief
le pantalon   pants, slacks
la pantoufle   slipper
le parapluie   umbrella
le pardessus   overcoat
le portefeuille   wallet
le pull-over   sweater
le pyjama   pyjamas
la robe   dress
la robe de chambre   robe
le sac   purse
le short   shorts
les tennis (*m.*)   sneakers
le T-shirt   T-shirt
la veste   jacket
le vêtement   article of clothing

s'habiller   to get dressed
se déshabiller   to get undressed
porter   to wear

Animals

l'agneau (*m.*)   lamb
l'aigle (*m.*)   eagle
l'âne (*m.*)   donkey
l'animal (*m.*)   animal
la baleine   whale
le bœuf   ox
le chameau   camel
le chat   cat
le cheval   horse
la chèvre   goat
le chien   dog
la colombe   dove
le coq   rooster
le crapaud   toad
le crocodile   crocodile
le daim   deer
l'écureuil (*m.*)   squirrel

l'éléphant (*m.*) elephant
la girafe giraffe
la grenouille frog
le lapin rabbit
le lion lion
le loup wolf
le mouton sheep
la mule mule
l'oiseau (*m.*) bird
l'ours (*m.*) bear
le perroquet parrot
le pigeon pigeon
le poisson fish
la poule hen
le renard fox
le requin shark
le serpent snake
le singe monkey
la souris mouse
le taureau bull
le tigre tiger
la tortue turtle
la vache cow
le veau calf

Insects

l'abeille (*f.*) bee
l'araignée (*f.*) spider
le cafard cockroach
la coccinelle ladybug
la fourmi ant
l'insecte (*m.*) insect
le mille-pattes centipede
la mite moth
la mouche fly
le moustique mosquito
le papillon butterfly
la puce flea
la sauterelle grasshopper
le ver worm

The Garden

le buisson bush
le chrysanthème chrysanthemum
la fleur flower
le gazon lawn
le géranium geranium
l'herbe (*f.*) grass
le jardin garden
le lilas lilac
le lis lily
la marguerite daisy

le muguet lily of the valley
l'œillet (*m.*) carnation
l'orchidée (*f.*) orchid
la pensée pansy
la rose rose
la tulipe tulip

tondre le gazon to mow the lawn
planter to plant
arroser to water

Trees

l'arbre (*m.*) tree
le bouleau birch
le cèdre cedar
le chêne oak
l'érable (*m.*) maple
le frêne ash
le marronier chestnut
le palmier palm tree
le peuplier poplar
le pin pine tree
le platane plane-tree
le sapin fir
le saule pleureur weeping willow

Studies

l'algèbre (*f.*) algebra
la biologie biology
la botanique botany
la chimie chemistry
la comptabilité accounting
le cours class, course
le dessin drawing
la géographie geography
la géométrie geometry
la gym(nastique) physical education
l'histoire (*f.*) history
l'informatique (*m.*) computer science,
    data processing
la langue étrangère foreign language
les maths (mathématiques) math
la matière school subject
la musique music
la peinture painting
la physique physics
les sciences science
la sténographie shorthand
la zoologie zoology

passer un examen to take an exam
réussir à un examen to pass an exam

The Office

le classeur filing cabinet
le dossier file
la machine à calculer adding machine, calculator
la machine à écrire typewriter
l'ordinateur (*m.*) computer

taper à la machine to type
classer to file
dicter to dictate

The City

l'aéroport (*m.*) airport
l'avenue (*f.*) avenue
le boulevard boulevard
le carrefour intersection
le cimetière cemetery
la circulation traffic
l'embouteillage (*m.*) traffic jam
le feu rouge red light
le feu vert green light
la gare train station
l'immeuble apartment building
le métro subway
le monument monument
le parc park
la petite ville town
la place square
le piéton pedestrian
le pont bridge
le quai dock, pier, street along a river
le quartier city district, quarter
la rue street
le sens interdit wrong way
le sens unique one way (street)
le square square (with garden)
le stade stadium
le trottoir sidewalk
la ville city

Buildings

la banque bank
le bâtiment building
la bibliothèque library
le café café
la cathédrale cathedral
le château castle
le cinéma movie theater
le commissariat de police police station

l'école (*f.*) school
l'église (*f.*) church
la fabrique factory
l'hôpital (*m.*) hospital
l'hôtel (*m.*) hotel
l'hôtel de ville (*m.*) city hall
la mairie town hall
le musée museum
l'opéra (*m.*) opera house
le palais palace
la poste post office
la prison jail
la synagogue synagogue
le théâtre theater

Stores and Shops

la bijouterie jewelry store
la blanchisserie laundromat
la boucherie butcher shop
la boulangerie bakery
la boutique boutique
la charcuterie pork-butcher shop
la confiserie candy store
la cordonnerie shoe repair shop
la crémerie dairy
la devanture storefront
l'épicerie (*f.*) grocery store
le grand magasin department store
la laiterie dairy
la librairie bookstore
le magasin shop, store
le marchand de chaussures shoe store
le marchand de journaux newspaper stand
le merchand de primeurs fruit and vegetable store
le marchand de vins liquor store
le marché market
la papeterie stationery store
la pâtisserie pastry shop
la pharmacie pharmacy
la poissonnerie fish market
la quincaillerie hardware store
le restaurant restaurant
le supermarché supermarket
le tailleur tailor shop
la teinturerie dry cleaner

faire du lèche-vitrine to go window-shopping

Transportation

l'autobus (*m.*)   city bus
l'autocar (*m.*)   intercity bus
l'avion (*m.*)   plane
le bateau   ship, boat
la bicyclette   bicycle
le camion   truck
l'hélicoptère (*m.*)   helicopter
le jet   jet
le métro   subway
la mobylette   moped
la motocyclette   motorcycle
le T.G.V. (train à grande
     vitesse)   high-speed train
le taxi   taxi
le téléférique   cable car
le train   train
le voilier   sailboat
la voiture   car

Journey, Trip

les bagages (*m.*)   luggage
le billet   ticket
le billet aller-retour   round-trip ticket
le bureau de voyages   travel agency
la douane   customs
l'horaire (*m.*)   schedule
le passeport   passport
la place   seat
le porteur   porter
la réservation   reservation
la valise   suitcase

enregistrer les bagages   to check the
     luggage
Bon voyage!   Have a good trip!

Professions and Trades

l'acteur (*m.*)   actor
l'actrice (*f.*)   actress
l'agent de police (*m.*)   policeman
l'architecte (*m. & f.*)   architect
l'avocat(e)   lawyer
le (la) banquier(ère)   banker
le (la) boucher(ère)   butcher
le (la) boulanger(ère)   baker
le charpentier   carpenter
le chauffeur de taxi   taxi driver
le (la) coiffeur(euse)   hairdresser
le (la) commerçant(e)   merchant

le (la) comptable   accountant
le (la) dentiste   dentist
le docteur   doctor
l'écrivain (*m.*)   writer
l'électricien(ne)   electrician
le facteur   letter carrier
le (la) fermier(ère)   farmer
le (la) fleuriste   florist
l'infirmier(ère)   nurse
l'ingénieur (*m.*)   engineer
l'instituteur, l'institutrice   teacher
le (la) journaliste   journalist
le juge   judge
le (la) mécanicien(ne)   mechanic
le (la) musicien(ne)   musician
l'ouvrier(ère)   worker
le paysan   peasant
le (la) peintre   painter
le (la) pharmacien(ne)   pharmacist
le (la) photographe   photographer
le (la) pilote   pilot
le plombier   plumber
le prêtre   priest
le professeur   professor, teacher
le (la) secrétaire   secretary
le soldat (la femme soldat)   soldier
le (la) vendeur(euse)   salesperson
le (la) voyageur(euse) de
     commerce   traveling salesperson

Governmental Titles

le président   president
le vice président   vice-president
le premier ministre   prime minister
le gouverneur   governor
le préfet   head of *département*
     (administrative division in France)
le sous-préfet   assistant to *préfet*
le maire   mayor

Metals

l'acier (*m.*)   steel
l'aluminium (*m.*)   aluminum
l'argent (*m.*)   silver
le bronze   bronze
le cuivre   copper
l'étain (*m.*)   tin, pewter
le fer   iron
le laiton   brass
l'or (*m.*)   gold
le platine   platinum

le plomb   lead
le zinc   zinc

Materials

le bois   wood
la brique   brick
le caoutchouc   rubber
le ciment   cement
le coton   cotton
la laine   wool
le marbre   marble
le plâtre   plaster
la soie   silk
la toile   linen
la tuile   tile
le verre   glass

Geography

la baie   bay
le bois   wood
la colline   hill
le continent   continent
la côte   coast
le désert   desert
la dune   dune
l'étang (*m.*)   pond
le fleuve   large river
la forêt   forest
l'hémisphère (*f.*)   hemisphere
l'île (*f.*)   island
le lac   lake
le marécage   swamp
la mer   sea
la montagne   mountain
l'océan (*m.*)   ocean
la péninsule   peninsula
le pic   peak
la plage   beach
la plaine   plain
le plateau   plateau
la rivière   small river
la terre   earth
la vallée   valley

Sports

la balle   small ball (tennis)
le ballon   large ball (football, soccer)
le base-ball   baseball
le basket-ball   basketball
les boules   bowling (French)
la boxe   boxing

la course   race
l'entraînement (faire de)   practice (to practice)
l'équipe (*f.*)   team
le football (le foot)   soccer
le footing   walking
le golf   golf
le hockey   hockey
le jeu   game
le jogging   jogging
la lutte   wrestling
le match   match
la natation   swimming
le patin à glace   ice skating
le patin à roulettes   roller skating
le ping-pong   Ping-Pong
le ski   skiing
le ski nautique   water skiing
le sport   sport
le tennis   tennis
le vol à voile   gliding

The Car

l'accélérateur (*m.*)   accelerator
l'air (*m.*)   air
la batterie   battery
le changement de vitesse   gears, transmission
le coffre   trunk
l'essence (*f.*)   gasoline
l'essuie-glace (*m.*)   windshield wiper
le frein   brake
le garage   garage
la graisse   grease
l'huile (*f.*)   oil
le moteur   engine
la panne   breakdown
le pare-brise   windshield
le pneu   tire
le pneu crevé   flat tire
le pneu de rechange   spare tire
le réservoir   tank
le rétroviseur   driving mirror
la roue   wheel
la station d'essence   gas station
la vitesse   speed
la voiture   car
le volant   steering wheel

conduire   to drive
tomber en panne   to have a breakdown

Holidays

*Noël Christmas
*Le Nouvel an New Year's Day
 Le Mardi gras Fat Tuesday (Shrove
   Tuesday)
 La Semaine sainte Holy Week
 Le Vendredi saint Good Friday
*Pâques Easter
*La Pentecôte Whitsunday
*Le Premier mai (Fête du
   travail) May 1st (French Labor
   Day)
*Le 14 juillet (fête nationale) July
   14th (Bastille Day)
*Le 15 août Assumption Day
*Le 11 novembre Veterans Day

*Official holidays in France.

Polite Phrases

Félicitations! Congratulations!
Bonnes vacances! Have a good
   vacation!
Joyeux Noël! Merry Christmas!
Bonne Année! Happy New Year!
Bonne chance! Good luck!
Amusez-vous bien! Have a good time!
Joyeux anniversaire! Happy
   birthday!
Bonne fête! Happy name day!
Merci. Thank you.

Index

Verb Index

This verb index will enable you to compare hundreds of commonly used verbs to the book's numerous verb tables. Each of the following groups of regular or irregular verbs provides the page numbers where the various verb tenses are discussed in the book. Each group is then followed by some of the most common verbs—and their definitions—that follow those patterns. By recognizing which verbs follow a certain pattern, you will greatly increase your vocabulary—all at a glance.

Regular Verbs

Regular verbs can be categorized into three major groups according to their infinitive form endings. These endings are *-er*, *-ir*, or *-re*.

-er Verbs

Regular *-er* verbs are conjugated in the same way as the verb *parler*. The various conjugations of *parler* can be found on the following pages:

infinitive, 6	*imparfait* (imperfect), 10
present, 7	*passé simple* (simple past), 11
imperative, 13	past participle; 16, 17
future, 11	present subjunctive, 23
conditional, 12	past subjunctive, 24

Some common *-er* verbs appear in the following list.

NOTE: Some verbs use the auxiliary *être* in compound tenses. This is indicated in parentheses. A few verbs use the auxiliary *avoir* when they are followed by a direct object, but use the auxiliary *être* when they are not followed by a direct object. This is also noted after the verb.

abandonner to abandon	**accompagner** to accompany
abonner to subscribe	**accorder** to grant
aborder to tackle, approach	**accrocher** to hang up
abriter to give shelter	**accuser** to accuse
abuser to abuse	**adapter** to adapt
accentuer to accentuate	**admirer** to admire
accepter to accept	**adopter** to adopt

adorer to adore
adresser to address
agréer to accept
aider to help
aimer to love, like
ajouter to add
allumer to light, turn on
amuser to amuse
apporter to bring
apprécier to appreciate
apprendre to learn
arrêter to stop, arrest
arriver to arrive (aux. *être*)
assister to attend
baisser to lower
bavarder to chat
blaguer to kid, joke
blesser to hurt
brancher to plug in, connect
brosser to brush
brûler to burn
cacher to hide
casser to break
cesser to cease
changer to change
chanter to sing
chauffer to warm up
chercher to look for
circuler to circulate, move along
coiffer to style (hair)
commander to order
comparer to compare
composer to dial
confier to entrust, confide
conseiller to advise
consoler to console
continuer to continue
coucher to put to bed
couper to cut
créer to create
crier to shout, yell
cuisiner to cook
danser to dance
déchirer to tear
décider to decide
déclarer to declare
déjeuner to have lunch
demander to ask
démontrer to demonstrate
dépasser to pass, exceed
déranger to disturb
déshabiller to undress

désirer to desire
dessiner to draw
détester to detest
dîner to have dinner
donner to give
échapper to avoid, escape
écouter to listen
embêter to annoy, bother
embrasser to kiss
empêcher to prevent
emprunter to borrow
enseigner to teach
entrer to enter (aux. *être*)
épouser to marry
étonner to astonish, surprise
étudier to study
éviter to avoid
excuser to excuse
expliquer to explain
exprimer to express
fâcher to anger (someone)
féliciter to congratulate
fermer to close
fêter to celebrate, party
fonder to found
fumer to smoke
gagner to win
garder to keep
gêner to bother, embarrass
goûter to taste
guider to guide
habiller to dress
habiter to live, reside
hésiter to hesitate
imaginer to imagine
indiquer to indicate
informer to inform
insister to insist
intéresser to interest
interroger to interrogate
inviter to invite
jouer to play
juger to judge
jurer to swear, vow
laisser to let, leave (behind)
laver to wash
louer to praise
manquer to miss, lack
monter to go up, take up (aux. *être*
  or *avoir*)
montrer to show
organiser to organize

oser   to dare
oublier   to forget
pardonner   to forgive
parler   to speak
passer   to pass, spend (time), take (exam) (aux. *être* or *avoir*)
peigner   to comb
penser   to think
porter   to carry, wear
pousser   to push
préparer   to prepare
présenter   to present
prêter   to lend
prier   to beg, pray
proposer   to propose
quitter   to quit, leave
raconter   to tell
recommander   to recommend
reculer   to back up
refuser   to refuse
regarder   to look at, watch
regretter   to regret
remarquer   to notice
remercier   to thank
rencontrer   to meet
renseigner   to inform
rentrer   to go back, take back in (aux. *être* or *avoir*)
réparer   to repair
respecter   to respect
ressembler   to look like

rester   to stay (aux. *être*)
retourner   to return (somewhere), turn over (aux. *être* or *avoir*)
réveiller   to wake up
rêver   to dream
risquer   to risk
sauver   to save
sembler   to appear, seem
séparer   to separate
skier   to ski
songer   to think, ponder
sonner   to ring
souhaiter   to wish
supporter   to bear
télécopier   to fax
téléphoner   to telephone
terminer   to finish
tomber   to fall (aux. *être*)
toucher   to touch
tourner   to turn
tousser   to cough
travailler   to work
traverser   to cross
tromper   to deceive
trouver   to find
tuer   to kill
utiliser   to use
vérifier   to check
visiter   to visit
voler   to steal, fly
voter   to vote

-ir Verbs

Regular *-ir* verbs are conjugated in the same way as the verb *finir*. The various conjugations of *finir* can be found on the following pages:

infinitive, 6	*imparfait* (imperfect), 10
present, 8	*passé simple* (simple past), 11
imperative, 13	past participle; 16, 17
future, 11	present subjunctive, 23
conditional, 12	past subjunctive, 24

Some common *-ir* verbs appear in the following list:

abolir   to abolish
accomplir   to accomplish
agir   to act
agrandir   to enlarge

atterrir   to land
bâtir   to build
bénir   to bless
brunir   to tan

choisir   to choose
élargir   to widen
finir   to finish
grandir   to grow
grossir   to gain weight
guérir   to heal
investir   to invest
maigrir   to lose weight
mincir   to get slimmer
nourrir   to feed
obéir   to obey
pourrir   to rot
punir   to punish

raccourcir   to shorten
rajeunir   to feel younger, rejuvenate
ralentir   to slow down
réfléchir   to think over
remplir   to fill (up)
réunir   to gather
réussir   to succeed
rôtir   to roast
rougir   to blush
saisir   to seize
unir   to join
vieillir   to grow old

-*re* Verbs

Regular -*re* verbs are conjugated in the same way as the verb *vendre*. The various conjugations of *vendre* can be found on the following pages:

infinitive, 6	*imparfait* (imperfect), 10
present, 9	*passé simple* (simple past), 11
imperative, 13	past participle, 16
future, 11	present subjunctive, 23
conditional, 12	past subjunctive, 24

Some common -*re* verbs appear in the following list.

NOTE: Some verbs use the auxiliary *être* in compound tenses. This is noted in parentheses after the verb. A few verbs use the auxiliary *avoir* when followed by a direct object but use the auxiliary *être* when they are not followed by a direct object. This is also noted after the verb.

attendre   to wait
défendre   to defend, forbid
descendre   to go down, take down
   (aux. *être* or *avoir*)
entendre   to hear
fondre   to melt
mordre   to bite

perdre   to lose
rendre   to return, give back
répandre   to spill, spread
répondre   to answer
tendre   to stretch, extend
tondre   to mow
vendre   to sell

Irregular Verbs

There are various types of irregular verbs. Contrary to a regular verb, which is characterized by a stem and an ending that remains constant in a given conjugation, the stem of an irregular verb may change within a given conjugation and its endings are often unpredictable.

-er Verbs

The various conjugations of irregular *-er* verbs can be found on pages 31 and 32. The compound tenses for irregular *-er* verbs are conjugated the same as those for regular *-er* verbs, or they follow the conjugations of the verbs from which they are derived, such as *tourner/retourner*.

Stem-Changing Verbs with *Accent Grave* Added to Mute *-e-*

The following stem-changing verbs have regular *-er* verb endings, but the mute *-e-* of the verb stem gains an *accent grave* in some of the conjugated forms. They follow the same conjugation patterns as the verb *acheter*, which can be found on page 32. Some of these verbs are:

acheter	to buy	**lever**	to raise
achever	to finish, complete	**mener**	to lead (someone)
emmener	to take away (someone)	**peser**	to weigh
geler	to freeze	**promener**	to walk (someone)

Stem-Changing Verbs with *Accent Grave* Replacing *Accent Aigu*

These verbs have regular *-er* verb endings, but the *accent aigu* over the *-e-* of the verb stem is replaced by an *accent grave* in some of the conjugated forms. They are conjugated in the same way as the verb *préférer*, which can be found on page 32. Some of these verbs are:

céder	to give in	**interpréter**	to interpret
célébrer	to celebrate	**posséder**	to possess
compléter	to complete	**préférer**	to prefer
espérer	to hope	**protéger**	to protect
exagérer	to exaggerate	**répéter**	to repeat

Stem-Changing Verbs with *Cédille* Added

These verbs have regular *-er* verb endings, but the *-c-* of the verb stem gains a *cédille* in some of the conjugated forms. They follow the conjugation patterns of the verb *commencer*, which can be found on page 31. Some of these verbs are:

annoncer	to announce	**menacer**	to threaten
avancer	to move forward	**placer**	to place
commencer	to start	**prononcer**	to pronounce
effacer	to erase	**remplacer**	to replace
lancer	to toss, throw		

Stem-Changing Verbs with *-e-* Added After *-g-* in the Stem

These verbs have regular *-er* verb endings, but a mute *-e-* is added to the verb stem in some of the conjugated forms. They follow the conjugation patterns of the verb *manger*, which can be found on page 31. Some of these verbs are:

arranger	to arrange	**manger**	to eat
bouger	to move	**nager**	to swim
changer	to change	**neiger**	to snow
corriger	to correct	**obliger**	to force, require
déranger	to disturb	**partager**	to share
exiger	to demand	**plonger**	to dive
infliger	to inflict	**voyager**	to travel

Stem-Changing Verbs with *-i-* Replacing *-y-* in the Stem

These verbs have regular *-er* verb endings, but the *-y-* of the stem becomes an *-i-* in some of the conjugated forms. Unless otherwise indicated, they follow the conjugation patterns of the verb *payer*, which can be found on page 32. Some of these verbs are:

employer	to use, employ	**essuyer**	to wipe, dry
ennuyer	to annoy, bore	**nettoyer**	to clean
envoyer/renvoyer	to send, send back, fire	**noyer**	to drown
essayer	to try	**payer**	to pay

-ir Verbs (Not *-iss*)

There are several patterns of conjugation for irregular *-ir* verbs. Their various conjugations can be found on the pages indicated next to each of the following verbs. The compound tenses for irregular *-ir* verbs are conjugated the same as those for regular *-ir* verbs, or they follow the conjugation patterns of the verbs from which they are derived, such as *dormir/endormir*. When a verb requires the use of the auxillary *être* in the compound tenses, this is noted in parentheses.

Irregular *-ir* Verbs Following the Conjugation Pattern of *Partir*

dormir	to sleep, 37	**ressentir**	to feel (pain or emotion), 40
endormir	to put to sleep, 37	**sentir**	to feel, smell; 40
mentir	to lie, 40	**servir**	to serve, 40
partir	to leave, 39 (aux. *être*)	**sortir**	to go out, 40 (aux. *être* or *avoir*)

Irregular *-ir* Verbs Following the Conjugation Pattern of *Ouvrir*

couvrir	to cover, 39	**ouvrir**	to open, 39
cueillir	to pick, 37	**recueillir**	to gather, collect; 37
découvrir	to discover, 39	**souffrir**	to suffer, 39
offrir	to offer, 39		

Irregular -*ir* Verbs Following the Conjugation Patterns of *Venir* and *Tenir*

devenir   to become, 42 (aux. *être*)
obtenir   to obtain, 42
revenir   to come back, 42 (aux. *être*)

tenir   to hold, 42
venir   to come, 41 (aux. *être*)

Courir and *Mourir*

courir   to run, 36

mourir   to die; 38, 39 (aux. *être*)

-*re* Verbs

The majority of -*re* verbs have some irregular forms in various tenses and modes. Most of them have an irregular past participle and subjunctive. The verbs listed below have at least some of these irregular forms. Their various conjugations can be found on the pages indicated next to each verb. When a verb requires the use of the auxiliary *être* in compound tenses, this is noted in parentheses.

comprendre   to understand, 40
conduire   to drive, 35
connaître   to know, 36
croire   to believe, 36
décrire   to describe, 37
déplaire   to displease, 39
détruire   to destroy, 35
dire   to say, tell; 37
disparaître   to disappear, 36
écrire   to write, 37
éteindre   to turn off, extinguish; 36
faire   to do, make; 38
inscrire   to enroll (someone), note; 37
lire   to read, 38
mettre   to put, put on; 38
naître   to be born (aux. *être*), 39

paraître   to seem, appear; 36
peindre   to paint, 36
permettre   to permit, allow; 38
plaindre   to pity, 36
plaire   to please, 39
prendre   to take, 40
promettre   to promise, 38
reconnaître   to recognize, 36
rejoindre   to join, meet; 36
rire   to laugh, 40
suivre   to follow, 41
surprendre   to surprise, 40
survivre   to survive, 42
traduire   to translate, 35
vivre   to live, 42

-*oir* Verbs

The -*oir* verbs have some irregular forms, which can be found on the pages indicated next to each of the following verbs:

devoir   to have to, 37
pleuvoir   to rain, 44
pouvoir   to be able to, 40

savoir   to know, 40
voir   to see, 42
vouloir   to want, 42

Auxiliary Verbs

The verbs *avoir* and *être*, which have irregular patterns of conjugation, serve as auxiliary verbs in compound tenses such as the *passé composé*. These verbs can be found on pages 34 and 51. Similarly, various irregular conjugations of the verb *aller*, which serves as an auxiliary verb for the near future, can be found on pages 35 and 51.

aller	to go	**être**	to be
avoir	to have		

Reflexive or Pronominal Verbs

These verbs are used when the action reflects back to the person doing it: *Je me lave* (I wash myself). The reflexive verb conjugations depend on whether they are regular *-er*, *-ir*, or *-re* verbs or irregular verbs. What distinguishes a reflexive verb from a nonreflexive verb is that the verb is preceded by a reflexive pronoun (*me*, *te*, *se*, *nous*, or *vous*), which corresponds to the subject of the verb. Any verb that admits a direct or indirect object may be used reflexively: *laver/se laver* (to wash/to wash oneself).

NOTE: All verbs used reflexively use the auxiliary *être* in compound tenses.

General instructions regarding the conjugations of reflexive verbs can be found on pages 21 and 22. Specific conjugation patterns for regular *-er*, *-ir*, or *-re* verbs or irregular verbs can be found on the pages indicated after each of the following verbs.

s'amuser   to have fun, 7
s'appeler   to be called, 32
s'arrêter   to stop, 7
s'asseoir   to sit down, 35
s'en aller   to go away, 35
s'endormir   to fall asleep, 37
s'ennuyer   to get bored, 32
s'habiller   to get dressed, 7
se blesser   to hurt oneself, 7
se brosser   to brush (one's hair), 7
se coucher   to go to bed, 7
se demander   to wonder, 7
se dépêcher   to hurry, 7
se déshabiller   to get undressed, 7
se fâcher   to get mad, 7
se faire mal   to get hurt, 38
se laver   to wash (oneself), 7
se lever   to get up, 32

se marier   to get married, 7
se passer   to happen, 7
se passer de   to do without, 7
se porter   to feel (health), 7
se promener   to go for a walk, 32
se rappeler   to remember, 32
se reposer   to rest, 7
se retourner   to turn around, 7
se réveiller   to wake up, 7
se sentir   to feel (health or emotion), 40
se servir de   to use, 40
se souvenir   to remember; 41, 42
se taire   to be quiet, 41
se tromper   to be mistaken, 7
se trouver   to be (located or found), 7
se vanter   to boast, 7

Reflexive or pronominal verbs may also be used for reciprocal actions to show action passing from one person to another: *se rencontrer* (to meet each other). The following verbs are commonly used in that fashion:

s'écrire   to write to each other, 37
s'entendre   to get along with each other, 9
s'offrir   to offer to each other, 39
se battre   to fight with each other, 35
se comprendre   to understand each other, 40

se donner   to give to each other, 7
se parler   to speak to each other, 7
se rencontrer   to meet each other, 7
se réunir   to meet with each other, 8
se téléphoner   to call each other, 7
se voir   to see each other, 42